THE NEW WEBSTER'S DESK REFERENCE

D1488161

THE NEW WEBSTER'S DESK REFERENCE

Donald O. Bolander, M.A., Litt. D.
Special Section on Canadian Law by
Stephen A.M. Cherhoff

Previously published as *The New Lexicon Library of Knowledge.*

BERKLEY BOOKS, NEW YORK

Previously published as *The New Lexicon
Library of Knowledge.*

This Berkley book contains the complete
text of the original hardcover edition.
It has been completely reset in a typeface
designed for easy reading and was printed
from new film.

THE NEW WEBSTER'S DESK REFERENCE

A Berkley Book / published by arrangement with
Lexicon Publications

PRINTING HISTORY
Berkley edition / August 1991

ISBN: 0-425-12884-9

Contents

CONTENTS

Chapter 1

EFFECTIVE LETTER WRITING

In commerce and industry, there are three kinds of contacts between business firms and their customers, suppliers, and others — *personal contacts, telephone calls,* and *letters*. By far the majority of business contacts are made by letter!

But good letter writing is equally important for those in education, government, fund-raising and other private organizations, clubs, church groups, and many others.

In the pages that follow you will be given a solid working knowledge of good letter writing. You will easily and quickly be able to understand the principles and techniques presented. However, you must then put them into practice in your own work or activities.

EVERY LETTER A SELLING LETTER

First of all, remember that your letters represent you, your company, or your organization to the recipient or reader. If the person has not met or talked with you, his or her opinion of you or your organization depends on the way they react to your letter.

If the reaction is favorable, you have sold yourself to the person. If the reaction is negative, you have not sold the reader your idea.

The fundamental principle of good letter writing, then, is this: **Every letter is a selling letter**. The aim of every letter is to sell one or more ideas. The one idea that should be included and sold in every letter is *good will*. Additional ideas included in the letter will depend upon the writer's purpose.

Of course, certain business letters are specifically called sales letters. They are designed to get an order or to aid in getting an order for some product or service. In the average business organization, sales letters are considered the most important of all. But consider the selling problem of the writer who must refuse an adjustment, refuse credit, or demand payment, but who still wants to retain the good will of the customer. He, indeed, has a difficult problem.

But letters other than business letters must sell, too. Fund-raising letters must convince the reader to send in a contribution. Letters from a club or other organization may be to sell the member on attending the next meeting or perhaps just to convey information. But even so, the letters are selling the value of the organization, its benefits, the pride the member can feel in the group.

Keep in mind, then, that all letters should have the aim of being silent salesmen of good will, but in addition a letter will usually include other ideas. How does a successful letter sell its ideas? It does so in two ways: first by its *appearance*, and second by its *contents*.

APPEARANCE OF THE LETTER

Letters, like salesmen and window displays, depend upon their appearance for a favorable first impression. If a letter is slovenly, carelessly written, or unattractive, it gives the same impression as a salesman with unshined shoes and unpressed clothes. If the appearance is not attractive, the potential customer may reject the messenger — whether by salesman or letter — before he hears or reads the message.

Based on the principle that every letter is a selling letter, the first rule of effective letter writing is that *the letter must be pleasing in appearance and correct in form.*

The appearance of your letter depends upon many things. The color and quality of stationery, the way the letter is set on the page, its form, the perfection of the typing — all these create the fleeting, but important, first impression.

So that you may recognize the main features of good mechanical layout of a letter, they are discussed briefly here. This discussion applies to all correspondence as well as business letters.

Page Arrangement:

1. A letter should be framed within its margins, with narrow margins for a long letter and wide margins for a short letter.

2. There should be a little more space at the bottom than at the top of a typed letter to balance it properly,

since the optical center of a page is slightly higher than the actual center.

3. The date should be placed close to the body of the letter rather than near the letterhead, either four or six spaces above the inside address, depending upon the length of the letter.

4. If a letter is more than one page, the heading of each subsequent page should show the name of the recipient, the page number, and the date as follows:

Mr. H. J. James   Page 2   June 30, 19__

5. Single spacing between lines is normally used rather than double spacing because single spacing is more economical and more attractive. When single spacing is used, two spaces are left between paragraphs.

Letter Styles:

As mentioned, a part of the success of any letter is its appearance. On the pages which follow, types of letter layout or format are shown. The *full-block* and *modified-block* are the most widely used. However, the *simplified* form is often used particularly when the letter is not addressed to a specific person.

Note: In business, a company may have a standard format which they want all typists to use. If so, follow company instructions.

EFFECTIVE LETTER WRITING

Full Block Format

```
_____(Date)


_____
_____(Inside Address)
_____
_____: (Salutation)


_____
_____
_____(Body)_____
_____
_____
_____(Body con't)_____
_____, (Complimentary Close)


_____(Signature)


___(Typist's initials)
___(Enclosure or cc: line)
```

The *full-block format* starts all writing at the left-hand margin. This makes it unnecessary to set tab stops for indenting the date line and the complimentary close. A colon is placed after the salutation and a comma is placed after the complimentary close.

Note: The above sample layout illustrates the typed portion only. This typed portion, of course, would be on a letterhead with white margins left, right, and bottom.

Modified Block Format

```
                              (Date) _____



_____
_____(Inside Address)
_____

_____: (Salutation)

_____
_____
_____(Body)_____
_____
_____
_____(Body con't)_____
(Complimentary Close) _____

                    (Signature) _____

___(Typist's Initials)
___(Enclosure or cc: line)
```

In the *modified-block format*, the date line and complimentary close and signature line are indented to the right. All other lines start flush left.

Note: Some writers also indent the first line of each paragraph five spaces. This is called *mixed style*.

EFFECTIVE LETTER WRITING

Simplified Format

_____(Date)

_____

_____(Inside Address)

_____

_____(Subject or Attention Line)

_____

_____
_____(Body)_____
_____
_____
_____(Body con't)_____
_____

_____(Signature Line-underline)
_____(Typed Name and Title)

___(Typist's Initials)
___(Enclosure or cc: line)

The *simplified format* is similar to the full-block format in that all items begin at the left margin. The salutation is replaced by a subject line or an attention line; e.g., Attention: Accounts Receivable Department.

OTHER LETTER ELEMENTS

Punctuation — The most widely-accepted style of punctuation uses no end punctuation for the date and address but retains the colon after the salutation and the comma after the complimentary close. Use this punctuation unless your company specifies otherwise. For complete punctuation rules, see the *Punctuation Rules* section of this handbook.

Postscripts — If you want to add a friendly personal comment or reminder as a handwritten postscript to a typed letter, by all means do so. Typewritten postscripts, although they should not be overused, are permissible and actually are very effective when used judiciously. Start the postscript at the bottom of the letter, three or four spaces below the signature line. Place it even with the left-hand margin or indent to conform with the other paragraphs.

Abbreviations — Good form forbids the use of abbreviations in the date line (Sept. 26, 19—) or in the address (St., W., Co.). Even though it takes a little more time to write out Street, West, and Company, the appearance of your letter is important enough to merit the extra effort. There is one exception to this no-abbreviation rule. If the corporate name of the company you are addressing contains the abbreviation *Co.* or *Inc.*, use it. Always use such widely accepted abbreviations as *Mr.*,

8

Mrs., *Jr.*, *Sr.*, *Dr.*, *D.C.*, and *St.* as in *St. Louis.* For more information, see the *Rules for Abbreviations* sections of this handbook.

Spelling — Be extremely careful to spell correctly the name of either a company or an individual to whom a letter is addressed. Verify spellings, if you have the slightest doubt.

Note: Elsewhere in this book you will find a complete presentation of *Spelling Rules*, a listing of commonly *Misspelled Words*, plus a special listing of *Words Confused and Misused*.

Spelling includes the correct division of words at the end of lines. The pronounciation of words governs their division or syllabication. Your reader might well be bewildered by such incorrect division as *daug-hter, cynical, progr-ess.*

Note: See the section on *Word Division* in this book.

Readability — Does your letter look inviting and easy to read? It won't, if it is composed of long, solid, difficult-looking paragraphs. Vary the length of your paragraphs. Usually they should not exceed ten lines. Don't be afraid of a one-sentence or two-line paragraph, especially if you want an important idea to stand out. Your sentences, too, should be short enough to read easily.

CONTENTS OF THE LETTER

The appearance of your letter is important because from it your reader gets his first impression of you and your message. But the contents are even more important in making sure that every letter is a selling letter.

Fundamentally, your letters will sell *only if they are written from the other person's point of view* rather than from your own. Much has been said and written — and properly so — about the "you" attitude in business letters, and it is equally important in social correspondence. There are still far too many letters which begin almost every paragraph with *I* or *we* because the writer is thinking of himself rather than the reader.

BE COURTEOUS AND CONSIDERATE

The "you" attitude is not merely an appeal to vanity or pride. If it were, it would be insincere and ineffective. The real "you" attitude is the ability to put yourself in the other person's place and to govern your actions — or write your letters — accordingly. This assures the sincerity that is essential to the effectiveness of any letter.

To accomplish your aim of making every letter a selling letter, therefore, your second rule is: *Be courteous and considerate*.

Certain words or phrases should never appear in a courteous, considerate letter. They invariably cause resentment and hostility by connotation, if not by denotation. Consider the words *you claim* or *your claim, you state* or *your assertion*. If you use these words, you might as well add, *but we don't believe you,* for that is the impression you will give.

Obviously is another word to shun as you would poison ivy, for it almost always has a bad effect on the reader. Here is an example from an adjustment letter which lost a valuable customer for a retail store: "Obviously you did not read our last letter carefully or you would have understood that the credit would be shown on next month's bill."

It didn't matter to the customer that her complaint was unjustified and that the adjustment had been made. She had been insulted by a discourteous correspondent who, in effect, had said, "If you're so stupid that you can't understand what we write, we'll just have to point out that *obviously* the credit will appear next month." The customer retaliated by sending back her credit card. Since her account had averaged more than $100 a month, this was truly an expensive letter.

How much better it would have been to say, "Our last letter evidently was not clearly expressed. We are glad to assure you that the credit will be shown on next month's bill. Thank you for writing us."

Evidently, apparently, and *manifestly* are other adverbs which should be used with care. Although you can safely say, *we evidently* or *we apparently,* don't say, *you evidently* or *you apparently.* Keep the other person's viewpoint in mind, and your letters will be courteous and considerate.

"Thank you" is one phrase that never becomes trite. You may say thank you in nine letters out of ten, and yet never sound stale to your reader. It is one positive way of putting the you before the I in your letters. How many letters do you receive or write which begin, "We have your letter . . . ." or "In response to your letter of . . . ." or even "On receipt of your letter . . . ."? If it is necessary to acknowledge the receipt of a letter — and in business it is sometimes helpful in keeping files in proper order — why not simply say, "Thank you for your letter of . . . ." or "Thank you for writing us about . . . ."?

This simple, natural way of expressing friendly appreciation illustrates the third rule in making every letter a selling letter: *Be informal and natural.*

BE INFORMAL AND NATURAL

There are varying degrees of formality in both written and spoken communication. Conversation is the most informal kind of spoken communication, and letters should be the most informal written communication. Personal letters are even more informal than business letters.

Conversation does not require the same degree of organization as the letter, and it has the added advantage of immediate give-and-take. The letter is documentary in nature (although it should never read like a legal document) and must await a reply. Although you cannot say everything in a letter that you would in conversation (the "Hi ya, Joe, whadda yu know" type conversation), you might safely follow this rule: If you wouldn't say it, don't write it — but don't write everything you'd say. Don't let the idea of writing become too high a hurdle. What you are really doing is *talking* to the other person — on paper.

TRITE WORDS AND PHRASES

To be natural and informal, watch your letters carefully until you have eliminated all the cliches — hackneyed, trite, old-fashioned words and phrases — which make a letter sound stilted and formal. You would never dream of using such a vocabulary if you were talking to the other person.

Would you in talking, for instance, use such obsequious language as *your kind favor, your esteemed favor, your obedient servant,* or *I beg to state*? These are hangovers from the nineteenth century. Many a modern, progressive business fails to sell its ideas by letter because of antiquated phraseology. In social correspondence as well, the artificially exaggerated expressions of courtesy have given way to friendly informality.

Approach all your correspondence with an analytical mind. If a word or phrase jars you, question its importance and meaningfulness. Ask yourself if you would use it in talking with the other person. If you would not, the word probably would not be effective in a letter, Apply the ''Would I say it?'' test with judgment, of course, remembering that you do not want your letters — except the most personal — to be chatty or intimate. You merely want them to be friendly and informal.

BE CLEAR AND CONCISE

Have your facts clearly in mind before starting to write. Otherwise, your reader may misunderstand, necessitating additional, expensive correspondence. The second letter is always more difficult to write, for it is harder to explain a misunderstanding which has arisen because of confused information than it is to say it right the first time.

The fourth general rule, then, to make every letter a selling letter is: *Be clear and concise*.

Take time to analyze the situation before you begin. Ask yourself, ''What do I have to say?'' Then marshal your facts, mentally or by penciled notation, and put your ideas in logical order. Finally, express what you have to say clearly and simply. When you read your mail, you may find it helpful to put small dots or question marks or even brief penciled notes in the margin opposite the sentences you want to answer. Then, when you are ready to reply, you will not need to reread the letter word for word.

If you are explaining or questioning several different items on a bill, or a number of insurance policies, or various steps in assembling a piece of machinery, use one paragraph for each item or each stem.

Test the clarity of your letter by reading it from the other person's viewpoint before you mail it. Does it answer every question? Does it anticipate those which might result from this correspondence? Is the information given in simple, clear, concise language?

Concise does not mean abrupt or curt. By definition, it means to express much in a few words. It means, therefore, that you should express your thoughts completely but briefly. Do not be disturbed if you find that a letter must be long to cover the information completely. A letter is not ineffective merely because it is long. It is ineffective if it is incomplete. Short letters are manifestly more economical than long ones, but don't make a letter short at the expense of courtesy or completeness.

For conciseness, try to eliminate from your letter the "cluttering" words — words which do not advance an idea. If you are doubtful of a word or phrase, ask yourself, "Does it advance the idea or hinder its advancement?" If it does not advance the idea, drop it! You will find that your ideas are more clearly expressed and your letters more interesting and effective.

INTRODUCTIONS AND CONCLUSIONS

An important aspect of letter writing is how to open and close your letter. Frequently you hear letter writers exclaim, "If I could just get started, I'd be all right" or "I wish I knew how to end this thing." It is true that a lame beginning or ending will detract from the effectiveness of a letter. A poor beginning fails to capture attention — the first essential of a good letter as well as a good speech. A weak ending will leave the other person feeling let down instead of stimulated to action as he should be.

TYPES OF OPENING SENTENCES

Here are some suggestions that will aid you in writing effective openings:

"Thank You" Opening — Like the salesman, you want to make your first words count. The beginning of a letter is the most important place to express the "you" attitude, and there is no better "you" than a "thank you." For example, *Thank you for your letter asking for information about our computer software programs.*

Positive Opening — Shun negative ideas in your openings, and minimize them as much as possible throughout your letter. Don't open a letter with *We are sorry to learn* or *It was most unfortunate*. For every negative there is a positive, and if you have made a mistake, the other person will be glad to know it has been corrected. Instead of apologizing, make positive statements such as *You will be glad to know* or *Fortunately, we were able to.*

Summary Opening — Try the journalistic approach. Summarize the facts or give the main idea in your opening sentence as is done in this example: *The adjustment you requested in your letter of October 10 has been made, and the credit will appear on your November bill.*

Question Opening — Don't be afraid to open with a question if it is natural and sensible to do so. For example, *Have you had an opportunity to consider the proposition we outlined in our letter of April 10?*

"Please" Opening — Use a "please" opening occasionally when it is important that you have immediate action. *Please give us the dates of the bills which are past due.* Or, *Please tell us when you returned the mer-*

chandise referred to in your letter of March 5 so that we can check our records.

"If" Opening — Does an "if" opening seem unusual? Because it is different, it is frequently effective in arousing attention and stimulating action. Watch for opportunities to use the "if" opening, as shown in these examples: *If you will give us the name of the salesman you wrote us about last week, we will check the order with him.* Or, *If you can come in to our office next week, we shall be glad to talk with you about the proposition you suggested in your letter.*

Remember that every sentence in your letter is important, but none is more important than the first sentence. It is there that you gain or lose the reader's interest.

TYPES OF CLOSING SENTENCES

Of only secondary importance to the opening is the closing sentence. Here is where salesmen apply what is known as the "hook," a slang term meaning *stimulus to action.* Like a firecracker which fails to explode, a letter which fizzles out is a "dud." Don't spoil the effectiveness of a letter with an ending that fizzles.

Use definite, to-the-point statements that are not high pressure but emphatic enough to induce action. Here is the place where the word *we* can be used to advantage. *As soon as we hear from you, we will,* or *If we can* *answer any questions, we shall be glad to do so.*

Avoid long, vague generalizations and negatives. Be sure to leave a clear idea of what you expect. You can do this by calling attention to some idea previously expressed, or by summarizing the main purpose of the letter, or by saving your most important idea for the last, as a climax to your letter.

Use questions. A question may formulate a courteous request such as, *Will you please give us this information before the end of the week?* Or, *Will you please handle this promptly?* Other questions might be, *Can you arrange to handle this shipment?* or *What is your opinion?* You can change the courteous request to a courteous demand by changing from the interrogative to the imperative mood. *Please give us this information* or *Please handle this.*

Avoid connections. The last sentence of your letter should never be connected with the complimentary close. Do not say, *Awaiting your reply, we are — Yours very truly.* It is also incorrect to say, *With best wishes, we are,* or *With kindest regards, we are.*

Because *Please accept my best wishes* sounds stilted, try to find some other friendly closing idea. Occasionally, when letter writers are close friends, just the words *best wishes* or *best regards* may be used as a breezy, personal closing. Such phrases should never take the place of the complimentary close in a business letter. They should be placed as a separate, final paragraph.

ANALYZING LETTERS

Now that you have considered the general principles of letter writing, you are ready to analyze and evaluate specific types of correspondence, both business and social. The most effective method of analysis is to ask questions that will train you to detect the good and bad points of any letter.

The following check list gives a series of questions that you should ask yourself about the specific letter which you are analyzing. This list is called the Four-A Check List since, when you are writing, you are concerned with the *aim, appearance, accuracy,* and *attitude* of a letter.

FOUR-A CHECK LIST
For Business and Social Letters

Aim
    a. What are the specific purposes of the letter?
    b. Does it accomplish these purposes?

Appearance
    c. Is the letter pleasing in appearance?
    d. Is it correct and consistent in mechanics according to the style used?

Accuracy

   e. Is the letter grammatical?

   f. Are spelling, syllabication, capitalization, punctuation, and abbreviations correct?

   g. Are the sentences and paragraphs varied in length?

   h. Are the ideas presented in logical order?

   i. Is the letter clear and concise? Does it include any irrelevant ideas or use any unnecessary words?

   j. Is the choice of words fully effective?

Attitude

   k. Does the letter have the "you" attitude — not merely through the use of the pronoun "you" but through ideas expressed from the other person's viewpoint?

   l. Does the letter have words that are negative or words that will have a bad effect on the reader?

   m. Does it include, whenever necessary, courteous expressions of thanks, appreciation, etc?

   n. Are trite or old-fashioned words and phrases avoided?

   o. Is the letter informal and natural in tone?

   p. Is abrupt or curt wording avoided?

   q. Does the closing thought leave the reader with the desired idea?

Using the Check List

You will find that the questions in the Four-A Check

List are easy to apply to any letter. When you begin to analyze your letters, have the check list open in front of you and check your letter carefully against each question in the list. You will soon be able to detect faults almost automatically and will need to refer to the list only occasionally.

LETTER PARTS

As discussed earlier in this section, the appearance of your letter creates either a favorable or unfavorable impression. Here is a brief explanation of the specific parts of a letter so that your letters conform to generally accepted usages.

Sender's Address: If you are writing on printed stationary, your name and address or the name of your company or organization is given on the letterhead. However, if you are writing a personal letter on plain paper, place your address immediately above the date line.

670 Walnut Street
Little Falls, NJ 07424
June 27, 19—

Date Line: Do not abbreviate dates. Spell out the month and do not use ordinals (*nd, rd, st, th*). Do not use the military version except in military correspondence.

No: 9/21/87
No: Sept. 21st, 1987
No: 21 September 87 (military)
Yes: September 21, 1987

Receiver's Address: Use the proper complimentary title (*Mr., Mrs., Ms., Dr.*) with the person's name, his or her position if known, and the name of the company or organization followed by the complete address.

Mr. Robert Costantini
Director of Publications
Hexagon Publishers, Inc.
1000 Lexington Avenue
New York, NY 10018

Apartment or suite numbers may be placed either on the same line with the address or if the address is too long, on a separate line immediately above it.

Note 1: For titles of educational, governmental, military, and religious dignitaries, see the *Forms of Address* section of this book.

Note 2: If writing to an individual at a home address, only the name and address would be given.

Salutations: The salutation should follow two spaces after the inside address. It is generally followed by a colon, but some writers omit the colon. The choice of the salutation depends on the relationship with the reader. Unless you know the reader quite well, use a moderately dignified salutation.

Recommended Salutations
Dear Mr. Henderson:
Dear Mrs. Chambers:
Dear Ms. Risner:

Salutations To Be Avoided
Dear Sir: Dear Madam:
Gentlemen: Mesdames:

If you are not writing to a specific person, use a *subject* line or *attention* line as explained for the simplified letter format.

Instead of a salutation some modern writers recommend an opening *attention getting phrase* which is generally part of the first sentence as follows:

It was great seeing you again, Tom . . .
. . . at the annual convention.

Thank you for the time . . .
. . . you gave me yesterday, Mr. Henderson, to review my qualifications.

It's true, Mrs. Jordan,
— It was our error. Your account has not been credited.

Body of the Letter: Begin the body of the letter two spaces below the salutation or subject line. Unless the letter is very brief, it should be single-spaced with a double space between paragraphs. If double spacing is used, the first line of each paragraph should be indented.

Complimentary Close: Complimentary closes should be followed by commas, capitalizing only the first word. Here are some accepted closes.

Sincerely,	Cordially,
Sincerely yours,	Best regards,
Very truly yours,	Regards,

The close *Respectfully yours* may be used for a top business executive, government official, or church dignitary. Other complimentary closes are given in the *Forms of Address* section of this book.

Signature and Writers Identification: Type the writer's name and title immediately below the complimentary close. Leave three to five spaces for the signature.

Sincerely yours,

Henry K. Peters
Director of Public Relations

Typist's Initials: The initials should be placed two spaces below the writer's title or name and flush left with the margin. The writer's initials need not be shown.

No: HKP: dob   *Yes*: dob

Enclosure Line: Use an enclosure line when other items are included in the letter. If there is more than one enclosure indicate the number. Place the enclosure line two spaces below the typist's initials.

Enclosure   Enclosures (3)

Carbon Copy Notation: If copies of the letter are being sent to other people note their names one or two spaces (depending on letter length) below the typist's initials or enclosure line. If necessary, give the person's title so the addressee knows his identity.

cc: Mr. Harry Rigio   cc: Walter Brown
     Ms. Jane Friedlan   Sales Coordinator

Chapter 2

FORMS OF ADDRESS

The following are preferred forms and correct use of titles:

Business Names and Titles

1. All titles in a business address should be capitalized. The "Zip" code should be placed two spaces after the state name without separating punctuation. Do not abbreviate *Company* or *Incorporated* unless the firm uses the abbreviations on its official letterhead.

Mr. John Rae, President
Graphic Products, Inc.
Monroe, Michigan 48048

Mr. Richard Greene
Chairman of the Board
General Dynamics Company
Quincy, Maine 02169

2. An educational or business title may be used with a personal title or degree for the same person.

Dr. Jay Howard
Director of Research
Dexter Electronics, Inc.

Thruman Hardwick, Ph.D.
Professor of History
Cornell University

3. A position title may be placed either on the same line, or on a separate line, based on length and convenience.

Mr. James Gordon, Superintendent
Riverdale Public Schools
Riverdale, Illinois

Mr. James Gordon
Superintendent of Schools
Riverdale, Illinois

4. The salutation *Gentlemen* may be used if the letter is not addressed to a specific person within the company, even though the letter is marked for the attention of that person.

Gould Incorporated
Chicago, Illinois
  Attention: Mr. Andrew Williams
Gentlemen:

Titles for Addressing Men

1. The title *Mr.* always precedes the name when addressing letters to a man, if he has no professional title.

Mr. Gary Jones
  or
Mr. Gary Jones, Manager

FORMS OF ADDRESS

Salutation: Dear Sir:
  or
Dear Mr. Jones:

2. For two or more men who have no professional title, *Mr.* should precede each name.

Mr. James North
Mr. Leo James

Salutation: Dear Sirs:
  or
Gentlemen:

3. The proper title for a boy under 12 is *Master*. From ages 12 to 18 usually no title is used. *Mr.* becomes the correct title at age 18.

Master Tommy Burns
Masters Tommy and Jim Burns

Salutation: Dear Tommy and Jim:

4. Designations such as Sr., Jr., III, etc., should be capitalized and usually are separated from the name by commas.

Mr. R.J. Hooker, Sr.
Peter Brady, Jr., Ph.D.
Dr. Arnold Smith, III

Mr. Raymond Gallo, Sr., President

Titles for Professional Men and Women

1. The title *Doctor* is designated for persons who have attained that degree.

Martin Gould, Ph.D.
  or
Dr. Martin Gould

Martha Merk, M.D.
  or
Dr. Martha Merk

Salutation: Dear Dr. Merk:

2. *Dr.* and *Mr.* should not be used with the same name.

Martin Gould, Ph.D.
  not
Dr. Martin Gould, Ph.D.

3. College or university teachers who hold professional rank are called *Professor* or *Prof.*

Professor Lenore Klein
  not
Professor Mrs. Klein

Professor Donald Boone
  not
Prof. Boone

FORMS OF ADDRESS

4. A professional man and his wife are addressed as:

Dr. and Mrs. Richard Warner
Professor and Mrs. James Donalson

5. The title *Messrs.* (*Messieurs*) precedes the name of two or more professional men jointly engaged in practice.

Messrs. Carl Bunker and Robert Black
Attorneys at Law

Titles for Addressing Women

1. The title *Miss* is used when addressing an unmarried woman. Authorities prefer the use of the title *Ms* for a woman whose marital status is unknown.

Miss Jean Peterson
Secretary to the President

Ms Shelly Streeter, Office Manager

Turner Supply Company

Misses is recommened when addressing two or more unmarried women.

The Misses Baker and Frederickson
The Misses Lena and Sarah Bronson

2. To address a married woman you should use *Mrs*. In business correspondence, the woman's personal first name is preferred. In social correspondence, her husband's name should be used.

> Mrs. Linda Reisman
>   (business)
> Mrs. John Reisman
>   (social)

For two or more married women *Mesdames* is used (or if one is married and one is single, *Mesdames* is also suggested).

> Mesdames Elyse Brown
> and Cynthia Birch
>
> Dear Ladies:
> Mesdames:
> Ladies:

3. The wife of a doctor or professor should not be addressed as Mrs. Dr. John Toomey or Mrs. Prof. B.T. Brown. The correct form is Mrs. B. T. Brown.

4. A divorced woman may use either her married name or her maiden name, and *Ms, Miss* or *Mrs.* are all correct. The preferred usage by the divorced woman should be followed.

FORMS OF ADDRESS

Military Titles

1. Military personnel should be addressed with the rank or grade held. If the military title contains a prefix as in Brigadier, the prefix may be omitted in the salutation. Military personnel may be greeted with Dear Sir: for example.

> Brigadier General Mark Reis, U.S.A.
> Address
> Dear General Reis:
>   *or*
> Dear Sir:

2. Naval commissioned officers below the rank of *Commander* may be addressed either with their rank or addressed as *Mr.* in the salutation.

> Lieutenant Fred Buckner, U.S.N.
> Address
> Dear Lieutenant Buckner:
>   *or*
> Dear Mr. Buckner:

The Complimentary Close

1. There are various complimentary closes which are acceptable for business correspondence. The preferred close is largely determined by the writer and the degree of friendliness he has with the person being written to. The first word of the close is always capitalized.

Sincerely,	Yours very truly,
Sincerely yours,	Respectfully,
Yours truly,	Respectfully yours,
Very truly yours,	Cordially,

2. Any of the following may be used for government officials:

Respectfully yours,	Very truly yours,
Respectfully,	Yours very truly,
Yours respectfully,	Sincerely yours,

3. For dignitaries of the church, any of the following may be used:

Faithfully yours	Yours in Christ
Respectfully yours,	Sincerely yours in Christ,
Respectfully,	Sincerely yours,

Chapter 3

TABLES OF ADDRESSES AND SALUTATIONS FOR GOVERNMENT, SCHOOL, AND CHURCH DIGNITARIES

Admiral (Four Star)
  Adm. Robert Stone, USN
  Address

  Dear Admiral Stone:

Ambassador, American
  The Honorable John Adams
  The American Ambassador
  Address

  Sir:
  Dear Mr. Ambassador:

Ambassador, Foreign
  His Excellency Ronald Scala
  The Ambassador of Italy
  Address

  Sir:
  Excellency:
  Dear Mr. Ambassador:

Archbishop (Catholic)
  Most Rev. Robert Carson
  Archbishop of (Ecclesiastical
    Province)
  Address

  Dear Archbishop Carson:

  The Most Reverend Archbishop
    of (Ecclesiastical Province)
  Address

  Most Reverend Sir:
  Your Excellency:
  Your Grace:

Archdeacon (Episcopal)
  The Venerable Alexander Roth
  Archdeacon of (Diocese)
  Address

  Venerable Sir:

  The Venerable Archdeacon
    of (Diocese)
  Address

  Venerable Sir:

Attorney General
  Hon. Charles Scott
  Attorney General of the State
    of (State Name)
  Address

TABLES OF ADDRESSES AND SALUTATIONS

Dear Mr. Scott

The Attorney General of the State
   of (State Name)
Address

Subject Line

Attorney
   Ms. Nancy T. Bell
   Attorney-at-Law
   Address

   Dear Ms. Bell:

Bishop (Catholic)
   Most Rev. Stephen Lewis
   Bishop of (Diocese)
   Address

   Dear Bishop Lewis
   Your Excellency:
   Most Reverend Sir:

Bishop (Episcopal)
   Right Rev. Gerald Berg
   Bishop of (Diocese)
   Address

   Dear Bishop Berg:
   Your Excellency:
   Right Reverend Sir:

Bishop, Other Denominations
Rev. Thomas Birch
Bishop of (Diocese)
Address

Dear Bishop Birch:

The Reverend Bishop Birch
Bishop of Memphis
Address

Reverend Sir:
Dear Bishop:
Dear Sir:

Brother
Brother James Dunne,*
LaSalle University
Address
*Add abbreviation of order

Dear Brother:
Dear Brother Dunne:

Cabinet Officer (Federal or State)
The Honorable Samuel Stern
Secretary of _____(State, etc.)
Address

Sir:
Dear Sir:
Dear Mr. Secretary:

TABLES OF ADDRESSES AND SALUTATIONS

Cardinal
　His Eminence Martin,
　　Cardinal _____
　Address

　Your Eminence:

Chancellor
　Dr. Patrick Bacon
　Chancellor of Pace University
　Address

　Dear Dr. Bacon:

　The Chancellor
　Pace University
　Address

　Subject Line:

Chaplin
　Chaplain Donald Folley
　Captain, U.S. Army
　Address

　Dear Chaplain:
　Dear Chaplain Folley:

City Council
　The City Council
　City of Toledo
　Address

　Honorable Sirs:
　Honorable Gentlemen:

Clerk of the Court
    Sally T. Brown, Esq.
    Clerk of the Court of Illinois
    Address

    Dear Ms. Brown:

    The Clerk of the Court of Illinois
    State Capital, State Zip

    Subject Line:

Colonel
Col. Terrence Black, USA (or USAF
    or USMC)
    Address

    Dear Colonel Black:

Commodore
    Com. Robert James, USCG (or USN)
Address

    Dear Commodore James:

Congressman or State Representative
    The Honorable Dean Shelly
    The House of Representatives
    Address

    Sir:
    Dear Mr. Shelly:
    Dear Congressman Shelly:
    (United States only)

TABLES OF ADDRESSES AND SALUTATIONS

Consul, American
  The American Consul
  (or: Gerald Dole, Esquire)
  American Consul
  Address

  Sir:
  Dear Sir:
  Dear Mr. Consul:
Consul, Foreign
  The Spanish Consul
  Address

  Sir:
  Dear Sir:
  Dear Mr. Consul:
Dean (Church)
  The Very Reverend Timothy Bello
  St. Patrick's Church
  Address

  Very Reverend Sir:
  Dear Dean:
Dean (College)
  Dean Gina Hawes,*
  LaFayette University
  Address
  *Add abbreviation of degree.

  Dear Dean (Dr.) Hawes:
  Dear Madam: (or Sir)
  Dear Dean:

General (Four Star)
> Gen. Richard Cornwall, USA
> (or USAF or USMC)
> Address

> Dear General Cornwall:

Governor
> The Honorable William Mason
> Governor, State of New Jersey
> Address

> Dear Sir:
> Dear Governor:

Judge
> The Honorable Daniel Galton
> Judge of the Circuit Court
> Address

> Dear Sir:
> Dear Judge:

Judge, Federal
> Hon. Nancy Bell
> Judge of the U.S. District
> Court of (District)
> Address

> Dear Judge Bell:

Mayor
> The Honorable Robert Benson
> Mayor, City of Richmond

TABLES OF ADDRESSES AND SALUTATIONS

Address
Sir:
Dear Mr. Mayor:
Dear Mayor:

Minister, American
Hon. Donald Brown
American Minister
Foreign City, Country

Dear Mr. Brown:

Minister, Foreign
Hon. Mary Marquette
Minister of (Country)
Washington, DC Zip

Dear Ms. Marquette:

Minister (Protestant)
The Reverend Jessie Burke
First Methodist Church
Address

Dear Sir:
Dear Doctor: (if D.D.)
Dear Mr. Burke:

Monsignor
The Right Reverend
  Monsignor Ben Stacey
  Name of Church
Address

Right Reverend Sir:
Dear Monsignor:
Right Reverend and
  Dear Monsignor:

The Pope
His Holiness, Pope ——
The Vatican
Vatican City, Italy

Your Holiness:
Most Heavenly Father:

Postmaster General
Hon. Victor Johns
The Postmaster General
Washington, DC 20540

Dear Mr. Johns:

The Postmaster General
Washington, DC 20540

Subject Line:

President (College or University)
William Buchner,*
President, Indiana University
Address
*Add abbreviation of highest degree.

Dear Sir:
Dear Mr. President:

TABLES OF ADDRESSES AND SALUTATIONS

President of the United States
    The President
    The White House
    Washington, D.C.

    Sir:
    Dear Mr. President:
Priest
    The Reverend Stephen Wilson,*
    University of Minnesota
    Address
    *Add abbreviation of order.

    Reverend Father:
    Dear Reverend Father:
    Dear Father:

Principal
    Dr. (Ms.) Martha Truman
    Principal of Paterson High School
    Address

    Dear Dr. (Ms.) Truman

Rabbi
    Rabbi Nathan Greene
    (or: The Reverend Nathan Greene)
    Sinai Congregation
    Address

    Dear Rabbi Greene:

    (With Doctor's Degree)
    Rabbi Nathan Greene, D.D.

(Name of Synagogue)
Address

Dear Rabbi (or Dr.) Greene:

Rear Admiral
Rear Admiral Dean Thelander, USCG
(or USN)
Address

Dear Admiral Thelander:

Rector
The Very Reverend Timothy Hart
Name of Church
Address

Dear Father Hart:
Very Reverend Sir:
Dear Reverend Hart:

Secretary of State (Treasurer
  or Commissioner)
Hon. Mark Andrews
Secretary of State of (State)
Address

Dear Mr. Andrews:

Senator (U.S. or State)
The Honorable Charles Nutley
United States Senate
(or: The State Senate)
Address

TABLES OF ADDRESSES AND SALUTATIONS

Sir:
Dear Senator:
Dear Senator Nutley:

Sister
Sister Catherine Mary,*
St. Elizabeth's Convent
Address
*Add abbreviation of order.

Dear Sister:
Dear Sister Mary:

Superintendent of Schools
Dr. (Mr.) Raymond McArdle
Superintendent of Glencoe City
  School System
Address

Dear Dr. (Mr.) McArdle:

Superior of Sister Order
Mother Teresa Mullens,*
Mother General
Address
*Add abbreviation of order.

Reverend Mother:
Dear Mother General:
Dear Sister Superior:

Supreme Court: Chief Justice
  Hon. Joseph Tiernan
  Chief Justice of the Supreme Court
  of (State)
  Address

  Dear Mr. Chief Justice:

Vice-President
  The Honorable Justine Smith
  The Vice-President of the
  United States

  Washington, D.C. 20025

  Sir:
  Mr. Vice-President:
  Dear Mr. Vice-President:

Chapter 4

IMPROVING YOUR SPELLING

To write a letter, report, or article that contains misspelled words is an almost unforgivable error. Frequent misspellings in business writing may prevent a person from being promoted to a position for which he or she is otherwise qualified. In high school or college a lower grade may be given to papers or reports that contain several misspelled words. Misspellings in social correspondence or in minutes, reports, etc. for club or church groups often affect a person's social or personal standing because errors create an impression of a lack of education or cultural background.

Suggestions for Improvement

Learning to spell well is not difficult, particularly if you set up a spelling improvement program for yourself. The program is simple and consists of the following steps:

1. **Learn the six basic spelling rules.** The rules are given on the following pages. The rules for forming plurals are also given.

2. **Keep a notebook of words you misspell.** Go over the words frequently until you are sure you know their correct spelling. You will be surprised how effective this

notebook system will be and how little of your time it will take. Continue keeping the notebook until you have learned to spell correctly the majority of words you regularly use in your writing.

3. **Don't guess about the spelling of a word.** Look up any word you are not sure of in a spelling dictionary or regular dictionary. If you find you have misspelled a word, add it to your spelling notebook. Looking up words in a dictionary takes a little time, but it prevents embarrassing mistakes.

In addition, immediately following this section you will find a list of 400 words which are frequently misspelled. Go over this list just as you do your notebook to help eliminate any errors you may now make. You will be pleased with how rapidly your spelling will improve.

SIX BASIC SPELLING RULES

Following are six basic spelling rules which will guide you in your program of spelling improvement. Each rule is illustrated by examples, and exceptions (if any) are noted.

Note: In another section of this handbook, a list of word roots, prefixes, and suffixes is given.

IMPROVING YOUR SPELLING

Rule 1. Words ending with a silent **e** usually drop the **e** when a suffix beginning with a vowel is added.

Root Word		Suffix		Complete Word
survive	+	al	=	survival
divide	+	ing	=	dividing
fortune	+	ate	=	fortunate
abuse	+	ive	=	abusive

Exceptions to the rule:

a. Words containing the soft sounds of **g** or **c** retain the **e** before the suffixes **able** or **ous**. *Examples*: Courageous, advantageous, peaceable, noticeable, changeable, manageable, serviceable.

b. Retain the **e** in words that might be mistaken for another word if the rule were applied. *Examples*: singe, singeing; dye, dyeing; shoe, shoeing; canoe, canoeing.

c. Words ending in **ie** drop the **e** and change the **i** to **y** when the suffix **ing** is added. This is done to prevent two **i**'s from coming together. Examples: die, dying; tie, tying; lie, lying.

d. In the words *mileage, acreage, lineage*, the **e** is not dropped before the suffix **age**.

Rule 2. Words ending with a silent **e** usually retain the **e** before a suffix beginning with a consonant.

51

Word		Suffix		Complete Word
arrange	+	ment	=	arrangement
awe	+	some	=	awesome
forgive	+	ness	=	forgiveness
safe	+	ty	=	safety
shame	+	less	=	shameless

Exceptions to the rule: judge, judgment; acknowledge, acknowledgment; argue, argument; true, truly; nine, ninth; pursue, pursuant; value, valuation; wise, wisdom; whole, wholly; awe, awful.

Rule 3. Words ending in a single consonant preceded by a single vowel, usually double the final consonant before a suffix beginning with a vowel.

run	+	ing	=	running
big	+	est	=	biggest
hot	+	er	=	hotter
plan	+	ing	=	planning
bag	+	age	=	baggage

If the word ends with two or more consonants, or if the final consonant is preceded by two vowels instead of one, the rule does not apply.

Two Consonants

debt	+	or	=	debtor
calm	+	est	=	calmest

Two Vowels

frail   + est = frailest
swear + ing = swearing
sweet + er   = sweeter

Rule 4. Words of two or more syllables, that are accented on the final syllable and end in a single consonant preceded by a single vowel, double the final consonant before a suffix beginning with a vowel. If the accent is not on the last syllable, the final consonant is not doubled.

Accent on Last Syllable

refer + ing   = referring
regret + able = regrettable
occur + ence = occurrence

Accent Not on Last Syllable

benefit + ed   = benefited
differ + ence = difference
travel + er   = traveler

If the word ends in two consonants, if the final consonant is preceded by two vowels, or if the accent shifts to the first syllable when the suffix is added, the rule does not apply.

perform + ance = performance
(two consonants)
repeal + ing = repealing
(two vowels)

refer   + ence = reference
(accent shifts)

Rule 5. Use of "ei" and "ie." Use i before e except when the two letters follow c and have a long e sound, or when the two vowels are pronounced long a.

Long e after c	Long a sound	After letters other than c
conceit	vein	shield
deceive	weight	believe
ceiling	veil	grieve
receipt	freight	niece
perceive	neighbor	mischievous

Exceptions to the rule:

weird	foreign	seize	leisure
either	forfeit	height	ancient
neither	sleight	surfeit	sovereign

Words that end in ie change the ie to y when the suffix ing is added.

lie - lying   die - dying   vie - vying

Rule 6. Words ending in y preceded by a consonant usually change the y to i before any suffix except one beginning with an i.

beauty   + ful   = beautiful
lady   + es   = ladies

lovely	+ ness	=	loveliness
ratify	+ es	=	ratifies
accompany	+ ment	=	accompaniment
accompany	+ ing	=	accompanying

Exceptions to the rule:

shy	+ ness	=	shyness
baby	+ hood	=	babyhood
plenty	+ ous	=	plenteous
lady	+ like	=	ladylike
beauty	+ ous	=	beauteous
wry	+ ly	=	wryly

If the final y is preceded by a vowel, the rule does not apply.

journey	+ s	=	journeys
buy	+ s	=	buys
essay	+ s	=	essays
obey	+ ing	=	obeying
repay	+ ing	=	repaying
attorney	+ s	=	attorneys

Note: This rule will be referred to later in the section on forming plurals.

FORMING PLURALS OF NOUNS

If a word is incorrectly pluralized, it is, of course, misspelled. There are thirteen rules on forming plurals listed here, together with examples and exceptions to the rules.

1. Plurals of most nouns are formed by adding **s** to the singular word.

Singular	Plural	Singular	Plural
bell	bells	pencil	pencils
college	colleges	tablet	tablets

2. When nouns end in **y** preceded by a consonant, the plural is formed by changing the **y** to **i** and adding **es**.

Final y preceded by a consonant:		Final y preceded by a vowel:	
Singular	Plural	Singular	Plural
baby	babies	valley	valleys
century	centuries	donkey	donkeys
lady	ladies	turkey	turkeys

Note: See Rule 6 under Basic Spelling Rules in this unit.

3. When nouns end in **ch, sh, ss, s, x,** or **z,** add **es** to form the plural.

Singular	Plural	Singular	Plural
dress	dresses	church	churches
fox	foxes	dish	dishes

4. The plurals of nouns ending in **f, ff,** or **fe** are formed by adding **s** to the singular. However, some nouns with these endings change the **f** or **fe** to **v** and add **es**.

Add s for plural		Change f to v and add es	
Singular	**Plural**	**Singular**	**Plural**
cliff	cliffs	wife	wives
handkerchief	hankerchiefs	leaf	leaves
safe	safes	self	selves

5. (a) The plurals of nouns ending in **o** preceded by a vowel usually are formed by adding **s** to the singular. Musical terms ending in **o** add **s** although the final **o** is not always preceded by a vowel.

Singular	**Plural**	**Singular**	**Plural**
studio	studios	piano	pianos
ratio	ratios	trio	trios
portfolio	portfolios	soprano	sopranos

(b) Nouns ending in **o** preceded by a consonant usually add **es** to form the plural.

Singular	**Plural**	**Singular**	**Plural**
motto	mottoes	hero	heroes
tomato	tomatoes	echo	echoes
potato	potatoes	Negro	Negroes

(c) Some nouns ending in **o** have two plural forms. In the following examples, the preferred plural form is given first:

Singular	**Plural**
memento	mementos or mementoes
cargo	cargos or cargoes
zero	zeros or zeroes

6. (a) Plurals of compound nouns are formed by adding s to the important word or most essential part of the compound.

Singular	Plural
sister-in-law	sisters-in-law
passer-by	passers-by
editor-in-chief	editors-in-chief
co-editor	co-editors

(b) Sometimes both parts of a compound are made plural.

manservant	menservants

(c) Compounds ending in **ful** form the plural by adding s to the ending of the compound.

Singular	Plural	Singular	Plural
cupful	cupfuls	handful	handfuls
spoonful	spoonfuls	tubful	tubfuls

(d) If there is no important word in the compound, or if both words are equal in importance, make the last part of the compound plural.

Singular	Plural
clothesbrush	clothesbrushes
scrubwoman	scrubwomen
washcloth	washcloths

7. Plurals of some nouns are formed either by a change in the vowel or by a complete change of spelling.

Singular	Plural	Singular	Plural
man	men	foot	feet
child	children	woman	women
mouse	mice	goose	geese
ox	oxen	tooth	teeth

8. Some nouns have the same form in both the singular and plural.

Examples: athletics, corps, deer, fish, moose, sheep, species

9. Some nouns are plural in form but are almost always considered to be singular in usage.

Examples: economics, ethics, news, mathematics, politics

10. Some nouns are rarely or never used in the singular.

Examples: cattle, cosmetics, scissors, statistics, trousers

11. Some words derived from a foreign language retain their foreign plurals.

Singular	Plural	Singular	Plural
datum	data	analysis	analyses
alumnus	alumni (masc.)	alumna	alumnae (fem.)
stratum	strata	synopsis	synopses

Sometimes, however, the English plurals are used instead of the foreign plurals.

Singular	Plural
referendum	referendums or referenda
curriculum	curriculums or curricula
trousseau	trousseaux or trousseaus

12. The plurals of proper nouns are formed by adding **s** if the name does not end in **s**, or by adding **es** if the name ends in **s**.

There are two **Marys** in our family.

Three **Besses** answered the roll call.

The **Adamses** have a new automobile.

The **Joneses** and the **Halls** are old college friends.

13. Plurals of letters, symbols, and numbers are formed by adding an apostrophe and **s** (**'s**).

Examples: A's x's 2's ?'s
+'s if's $'s 100's

FORMING POSSESSIVES

The apostrophe (') is a mark to show that a noun (or indefinite pronoun) is possessive, or to indicate a contraction. Just as a word is misspelled if it is pluralized incorrectly, so is it misspelled if the apostrophe is omitted or inserted in the wrong place in a word that shows possession.

1. If the singular form of the noun does not end in **s**, add the apostrophe and **s** ('s). If the singular ends in **s**, add the apostrophe (').

Note: In the possessive singular of nouns that end in **s**, if you want the sound of an additional **s**, the apostrophe and **s** ('s) may be added.

Singular	Possessive	Singular	Possessive
boy	boy's	Harold	Harold's
child	child's	woman	woman's
Ross	Ross'	Davis	Davis'
	(or Ross's)	(or Davis's)	

2. If the plural does not end in **s**, add the apostrophe and **s** ('s). If the plural ends in **s**, add the apostrophe (').

Helpful hint: Make the word plural first; then make it possessive.

Plural	Possessive	Plural	Possessive
calves	calves'	bosses	bosses'
boys	boys'	children	children's
men	men's	sheep	sheep's
weeks	weeks'	Joneses	Joneses'

Caution: Be sure that you always add the apostrophe to the end of a word and that you do not insert it within the word. For example, take the proper name Jones. If you insert the apostrophe before the **s** (Jone's), it would mean that the proper name was Jone.

3. Possessive personal pronouns do not require an apostrophe.

my, mine	you, your
he, his	we, ours
she, hers	they, theirs
it, its	who, whose

Note: *It's* is a contraction of *it is* not the possessive of *it*.

4. Possessives of indefinite pronouns are formed by adding an apostrophe and **s('s)**.

else's	someone's	everybody's
somebody's	everyone's	one's

5. Possession of a compound word is shown at the end of the word, regardless of which part of the compound

may be pluralized.

Singular	Singular Possessive
tradesman	tradesman's
editor-in-chief	editor-in-chief's
secretary-treasurer	secretary-treasurer's

Plural	Plural Possessive
brothers-in-law	brothers-in-law's
menservants	menservants'
freshmen	freshmen's

FORMING CONTRACTIONS

The second use of the apostrophe is to show the omission of one or more letters in words that are contracted.

it's (it is)	wouldn't (would not)
can't (cannot)	haven't (have not)
don't (do not)	hadn't (had not)
I've (I have)	isn't (is not)
I'm (I am)	you're (you are)
doesn't (does not)	won't (will not)
couldn't (could not)	who's (who is)

Chapter 5

440 WORDS
FREQUENTLY MISSPELLED

In business letters and reports and in reports or papers prepared by students in high school and college, there are certain words which are misspelled more often than others. Following is a list of words which are frequently misspelled. Refer to the list if you are unsure of the spelling of a word. If the word you are seeking is not in the list and you still are not sure, refer to a spelling dictionary or a regular dictionary.

abeyance	acquaintance
absence	acquisition
abundance	acquitted
accelerate	across
acceptable	actually
acceptance	advantageous
accessible	advisable
accidentally	aggravate
accommodate	aggressive
accompanying	allege
accomplish	allowance
accumulate	amendment
accurate	among
accustom	analysis
achievement	analyze
acknowledgment	announce
acknowledging	annoyance

apologize
apparatus
apparent
appealing
appearance
appreciate
approach
appropriate
argument
arrangement
ascertain
assessment
assistant
association
attendance
attorney
automatically
auxiliary
available
bankruptcy
bargain
beginning
belief
believe
believing
belligerent
beneficial
beneficiary
benefited
bookkeeping
budget
bulletin

bureau
business
calendar
cancel
canceled
cancellation
candidate
capital
capitol
career
catalog
category
certain
changeable
chargeable
collateral
collectible
column
commission
commitment
committed
committee
commodities
comparatively
competent
competition
concede
conceivable
conferred
confidence
confidentially
consummation

controlled
conscience
conscientious
conscious
consistent
conspicuous
continuously
controlling
controversial
counterfeit
convenient
conversant
convincing
correlation
correspondence
courteous
criticism
criticize
crucial
debtor
deceive
deductible
defendant
deferred
deficiency
deficit
definite
dependent
description
desirable
despair
detrimental

develop
difference
disappearance
disappoint
disastrous
disbursement
discipline
discussion
dissatisfaction
distribute
divide
efficiency
efficient
eighth
either
elaborate
eligible
eliminate
embarrass
eminently
emphatically
encouraging
endeavor
enforceable
enthusiastic
entirely
environment
equipment
equipped
equivalent
erroneous
especially

exaggerate
exceed
excellent
exhaustible
exhibition
existence
existent
exorbitant
expense
experience
explanation
extension
extraordinary
facilities
familiar
feasible
February
finally
financially
financier
forbade
foreign
forfeit
forty
forward
foresee
fourth
freight
fulfill
generally
government
grammar

grateful
guidance
handling
happiness
harass
height
hierarchy
hindrance
hurriedly
hygiene
image
immediately
immensely
imminent
impossible
incidentally
incredible
independent
indispensable
inevitable
influence
install
insistence
integrity
intelligence
intelligent
intentionally
interfere
interrupt
irrelevant
itinerary
judgment

judiciary
knowledge
knowledgeable
labeled
laboratory
laissez-faire
legible
legitimate
leisure
liable
liability
license
likable
likely
liquidate
lucrative
lying
maintenance
manageable
management
maneuver
manual
manufacturer
meant
mileage
millionaire
miniature
minute
miscellaneous
misspelled
monotonous
moral

morale
mortgage
movable
necessary
negligible
negotiate
neither
ninety
ninth
noticeable
oblige
obstacle
occasionally
occupant
occur
occurred
occurrence
offered
omission
omitted
oneself
operate
opinion
opportunity
ordinance
originally
paid
pamphlet
parallel
partially
particularly
pastime

patient
patronize
perceive
permanent
permissible
perseverance
personnel
persuade
pertain
pertinent
physically
plausible
pleasant
policies
possession
possible
possibly
practical
practically
precede
predictable
predominant
prejudice
prefer
preferable
preference
preferred
preparation
prerogative
presumptuous
prevalent
principal

principle
privilege
probably
procedure
proceed
programmed
programmer
propaganda
proportion
psychology
pursue
quality
quantity
questionnaire
realize
recede
receipt
receivables
receive
recipient
recognize
recommend
recruit
refer
reference
referred
regrettable
relevant
relieve
repetition
representative
requirement

rescind
research
resistance
responsibility
restaurant
rhythm
ridiculous
sacrifice
safety
salable
salient
schedule
secretary
seize
separate
severely
signature
significant
similar
simultaneous
sincerely
sizeable
skillful
source
specialized
specifically
strenuous
subtle
subtlety
succeed
success
suffered

sufficient
summarize
superintendent
supersede
supplies
suppress
surely
surprise
susceptible
symmetrical
sympathize
technique
temperament
temperature
temporarily
tendency
therefore
thorough
through
totaled
toward
transferred
transferring
transient
tremendous
typical
unanimous
undoubtedly
unnecessary
unusual
unwieldy
usage

440 WORDS FREQUENTLY MISSPELLED

useful
usually
vacillate
vacuum
valuable
variable
various
vegetable
vengeance
vice versa
victim
voluntary

warehouse
warrant
Wednesday
weather
weight
whether
wholly
write
writing
written
yield

Chapter 6

WORDS OFTEN CONFUSED
AND MISUSED

Many words, for whatever reason, are often confused with another word and therefore misused. Sometimes the words look or sound somewhat alike, or they may have a somewhat similar meaning but have different accepted usages. Following are words often confused and misused. Examples of the correct use of the words is given following the definitions.

accept -- except:
> *Accept* means to receive or to agree to something.
> > He did not *accept* the position.
> *Except* means to exclude or leave out.
> > Everyone *except* John is here.

adapt -- adept -- adopt:
> *Adapt* means to adjust to or to modify.
> > She did not *adapt* to her new job.
> *Adept* means skillful.
> > She is an *adept* typist.
> *Adopt* means to embrace or accept.
> > We will *adopt* a child.
> > They *adopted* the plan.

advice -- advise:

Advice is a noun meaning a recommendation that is given.

He gave me his *advice*.

Advise is a verb meaning an act of guidance.

Advise her what she should do.

affect -- effect:

Affect is a verb meaning to influence.

His attitude will *affect* his chances.

Effect is a noun indicating result or outcome.

What *effect* will the new plan have?

Effect is occasionally used as an action verb meaning to bring about.

We did *effect* your instructions.

aggravate -- irritate:

Aggravate means to make worse (a situation or condition).

His actions *aggravated* the situation.

The rubbing *aggravated* the wound.

Irritate means to annoy or to make sore.

The loud noise *irritated* me.

My skin is quite *irritated*.

allusion -- delusion -- illusion:

Allusion is an indirect reference to something.

She made an *allusion* to the mistake.

Delusion is a false or irrational belief.

He had a *delusion* that he would be made president.
He had *delusions* that he was being persecuted.
Illusion is a wrong idea or concept, or an optical misconception (In some usages, illusion and delusion mean about the same).

He had the *illusion* that he was to become president.
The mirage was strictly an *illusion*.

all ready -- already:
All ready means all prepared, i.e., a state of readiness.
The students were *all ready* to go.
Already is an adverb meaning previously.
The students had *already* gone.

all together -- altogether:
All together means a group as a whole.
The tools were *all together* on the bench.
Altogether means completely.
The two plans were *altogether* different.

among -- between:
Among is used when more than two persons or things are involved.
The supplies were divided *among* the group.
Between is used when only two persons or things are involved.
Jim and Ed divided the supplies *between* them.

amount -- number:

Amount, except for money, is used when mentioning something that cannot be counted.

The bill *amounted* to $64.50.

She had a large *amount* of cash.

He has a great *amount* of courage.

Number is used for things that can be counted.

A *number* of dogs were in the kennel.

A great *number* voted "no".

anxious -- eager:

Anxious means to have a degree of anxiety or fear.

I am *anxious* to hear the results of the operation.

Eager means pleasant anticipation.

I am *eager* to meet her.

any one -- anyone:

Any one is used to refer to one of several things or persons.

I do not like *any one* of the plans.

Any one who wishes may go.

Anyone is a pronoun meaning any person.

Has *anyone* arrived yet?

avenge -- revenge:

Avenge is used when there is a moral intention to right a wrong.

I will try to *avenge* the injustice done to him.

75

Revenge is a desire to inflict a punishment for an insult or injury.

He is so angry that he is going to seek *revenge*.

bad -- badly:

Bad is an adjective meaning disagreeable, offensive, defective.

Mother feels *bad* this morning.

The sales results were very *bad*.

There is a *bad* odor in the room.

Badly is an adverb meaning in a bad manner.

He behaved *badly* at the meeting.

best -- better:

Best is used when comparing more than two persons or things.

His plan was the *best* of those submitted.

Better is used when comparing two people or things.

His plan is the *better* of the two.

borrow -- lend:

Borrow means that the person is taking or wishes to take.

May I *borrow* your car?

Lend means to give or to let use.

I am going to *lend* him my car.

can -- may:

Can means to be able or capable of doing something.

He *can* operate the machine. (is able to)
Can he operate the machine? (does he know how?)
May means to seek or give permission.
He *may* operate the machine. (giving permission)
May he operate the machine? (seeking permission)

capital -- capitol:
Capital refers to a city where a national, state, or province government is located; also to monetary possessions, including money.
Washington, D.C. is the *capital* of the United States.
He invested most of his *capital* (money) in the new company.
Capitol refers to the main government building.
His office is in the *capitol*. (building)

complement -- compliment:
Complement refers to people or things that go well or work well together.
The advertising program *complemented* the increased sales effort.
Compliment means to praise.
They *complimented* us on the increased sales.

counsel -- council -- counsul:
Counsel as a verb means to give advice; as a noun it

means a lawyer or other person who gives advice.

He *counseled* us on the strategy we should use.

He is our company legal *counsel*.

Council is a group of people who discuss and/or take action on various matters.

The city *council* is meeting today.

Counsul is a government official appointed to represent citizens of his country in a foreign country.

The new *counsul* is leaving for Mexico tomorrow.

continual -- continuous:

Continual refers to something that occurs regularly, but with interruption.

His *continual* complaints are irritating.

Continuous means something that occurs without pause.

The *continous* noise in the shop is irritating.

emigrate -- immigrate:

Emigrate means to leave one's country to settle in another.

To avoid political persecution, he *emigrated* from Russia.

Immigrate means to enter a new country to settle there.

Because of political persecution, he *immigrated* to the United States.

eminent -- imminent:
Eminent means prominent or distinguished.
He is an *eminent* author.
Imminent means about to occur or threatening to occur.
A strike appeared to be *imminent*.

fewer -- less:

Fewer is used for things that can be counted.
We have had *fewer* plant accidents this year.
Less is used for things or ideas that cannot be counted.
He is *less* qualified than she is.

farther -- further:
Farther pertains to distance.
How much *farther* do we have to go?
Further refers to degree or extent but not to distance.
She can go no *further* in that type of work.

good -- well:
Good is an adjective that describes something positive.
She has a *good* educational background.
Well is an adjective meaning skillful, satisfactory, or thorough. It is also used to describe a state of health.
He is doing *well* in his new job.

The office manager does not look *well* today.

imply -- infer:
Imply means a hint or indirect suggestion.

He *implied* that he was going to quit.

Infer means to draw a conclusion from or interpret the meaning.

From what he said, I *infer* he may quit.

in -- into:
In indicates that something is already at a place or location.

The computers are *in* the next room.

Into indicates that someone or something is moving from the outside to the inside of a place.

He went *into* the computer room.

lay -- lie:
Lay means to put something down, to place something somewhere.

The principal parts are *lay*, *laid*, (*have*, *has*, or *had*) *laid*.

The present participle form is *laying*. The verb *lay* always takes an object.

He *lays* tile for the Regal store.

He *laid* tile for the Petersons.

He *has laid* tile for our neighbors.

He is *laying* tile today.

(Tile is the object of all the above sentences.)

Lie means to recline, to rest, or to remain in a reclining position.

The principal parts are *lie*, *lay*, (*have*, *has had*) *lain*. The present participle form is *lying*.

He *lies* down every afternoon.

He *lay* on the couch all afternoon.

He *has lain* on the couch at times.

He *is lying* on the couch.

The verb *lie* is also the verb to use when speaking of inanimate objects that are in a reclining or in a *lying-down* position.

The report *lies* on my desk.

The report *lay* on my desk for a week.

The report *has lain* on my desk for weeks.

The report *is lying* on my desk.

There is another verb *lie* which means falsehood. It causes no special problems. Its principal parts are *lie*, *lied*, *lying*.

learn -- teach:

Learn indicates that knowledge or behavior is being acquired.

He should *learn* from that experience.

He *learned* Spanish in college.

Teach indicates that knowledge is being provided.

That experience should *teach* him a lesson.

He was *taught* conversational Spanish in college.

liable -- likely:

Liable is used either to indicate legal responsibility or the likelihood of an undesirable possibility.

If you injure someone, you are *liable* for damages.

If you don't change your ways, you are *liable* to be fired.

Likely indicates the probability of something.

She is *likely* to be the next one promoted.

It is *likely* you will be fired if you don't change your ways.

precede -- proceed:

Precede means to come or go before someone or something.

The band will *precede* the float.

Careful investigation should *precede* any action.

Proceed means to go on, usually after an interruption.

We can now *proceed* with the plan.

principal -- principle:

Principal means 1) something that is most important, 2) the amount of money owed or invested, 3) the head officer of a school, 4) the employer of a person to act in his behalf.

The *principal* purpose of the plan is to reduce expenses.

The *principal* amounts to $100,000.

She is *principal* of the Bergen Grade School.
The lawyer did his best to protect the interests of his *principal*.
Principle is used to indicate a law, basic truth, rule of conduct, or guidance.

Democracies are based on the *principle* of self-government.
The *principles* of his religion govern his action.

quite -- quiet:
  Quite is an adverb meaning completely or very.
    The new plan is not *quite* ready.
    I am *quite* sure he will agree.
  Quiet means still, calm, motionless, silent.
    After hearing the announcement, the audience remained *quiet*.

raise -- rise:
  Raise means to lift or raise. It requires an object.
    Those who agree, *raise* your hand.
    We will have to *raise* our prices.
  Rise means to get up or go up. It requires no direct object.
    Please *rise* when the President enters.
    The audience *rose* (stood up) when the President arrived.
    Our taxes seem to *rise* every year.

set -- sit:

Set means to put something down or in a certain place, or to bring to a specified state or condition.

He *set* the books on the president's desk.

The trees were *set* on fire.

She has *set* her heart on going.

Sit means to be seated.

Please do not *sit* on the desk.

stationary, stationery:

Stationary means inmovable, not moving, or unchanging.

Once the machine is installed, it will be *stationary*.

The troops stood *stationary* until the flag was past.

Stationery refers to writing paper, envelopes, and other office supplies.

Our new *stationery* order has just arrived.

whose -- who's:

Whose is an adjective showing possession.

He is the one *whose* car was stolen.

Who's is a contraction of *who* and *is*. In writing, its use should be avoided.

Who's going to be at the meeting?

Chapter 7

WORD PREFIXES, SUFFIXES, AND ROOTS

Following are some of the important word prefixes used in English. The prefix is indicated in boldface type followed by the basic meaning of the prefix. Examples of the prefixes used in words are given in italic type.

ab-, a-, abs-, away from, *abduct, avert, abstain*

a-, an-, not, less, without, *agnostic, atheist, anarchy*

ad-, a-, ac-, af-, to, toward, *adhere, ascribe, accord, affirm*

ag-, al-, an-, *aggressor, allude, annex*

ap-, ar-, as-, at-, to, toward, *associate, attend*

ante-, before, *antedate, antecedent*

anti-, ant-, against, *antiseptic, antipathy, antacid*

ana-, up, through, throughout, *analysis, anatomy*

be-, by or near, *below, beside*

bene-, good, well, *benevolent, beneficial*

bi-, two, twice, *bicycle, biennial*

circum-, around, all round, *circumstance, circumvent*

com-, con-, col-, together, *combine, confound, collate*

contra-, against, *contradict, contravene*

de-, from, down away, *depart, descend, denude*

dis-, di-, apart, apart from, *distract, divert*

ex-, ef-, e-, out, out of, *export, effect, emit*

hypo-, under, beneath, *hypodermic, hypothesis*

in-, in, into, *intrude, inside, include, insight*

in-, im-, il-, ir-, un-, not, *inactive, impress, illicit, irrestible, unreal*

inter-, between, *intermingle, interstate*

intra-, intro-, within, *intramural, introduction*

mal-, bad, *malcontent, malnourished*

mis-, wrong, *misdeed, mislead*

non-, not, *nonentity, nonconformist*

ob-, against, *object, objective*

par-, para-, beside, beyond, *paradox, parallel*

per-, through, throughout, *persist, pervade*

peri-, around, *periscope, perimeter*

post-, after, *postpone, postscript*

pre-, before, *prefer, predict*

pro-, before, forward, *prologue, promote, pronoun*

re-, back, again, *refer, report, review*

retro-, backward, *retroactive, retrogress*

se-, apart, *seduce, sedate*

semi-, half, *semicircle, semiconscious*

sub-, under, *submit, subordinate*

super-, supra-, above, over, *supernatural, suprarational*

syn-, sym-, with, *synopsis, symphony, synonym*

trans-, tra-, across, *transfer, traverse*

un-, not, reversal of action, *uncovered, untie*

uni-, single, *unity, universal*

WORD PREFIXES, SUFFIXES AND ROOTS

vice-, instead of, *vice-president, vice-consul*
with-, against, back, *withdraw, withhold*

Word Suffixes

Following are some of the important word suffixes used in English. The suffix is indicated in boldface type followed by the basic meaning of the suffix. Examples of the suffixes used in words are given in italic type.

-able, -ible, -ble, capable of being, as *bearable, reversible, voluble*
-ac, -ic, pertaining to, as *cardiac, angelic*
-ac, -ic, condition or quality of, as *maniac, mechanic*
-acious, characterized by, as *pugnacious, tenacious*
-acity, quality of, as *tenacity, veracity*
-acy, having the quality of, as *accuracy, fallacy*
-age, collection of, state of being, as *garbage, marriage, storage*
-al, -el,-le, pertaining to, as *fanatical, novel, single*
-an, -ian, belonging to, one who, as *American, physician, historian*
-ance, relating to, as *reliance, distance*
-ancy, -ency, denoting state or quality, as *occupancy, dependency*
-ant, -ent, one who, as *tenant, correspondent*
-ar, -ary, ory, relating to, as *popular, dictionary, mandatory*

-ate, act, as *mandate, confiscate*
-ation, action, as *elation, separation*
-cle, -ule, -ling, diminutive, as *article, globule, suckling*
-cracy, rule, as democracy, autocracy
-cy, quality, as *idiocy, ascendency*
-dom, state of being, as *freedom, kingdom*
-ee, one who is acted upon, as *employee, trustee*
-ence, relating to, as *confidence, abstinence*
-er, -or, -ar, one who, as *butler, actor, scholar*
-ful, abounding in, as *grateful, sinful*
-fy, -efy, -ify, to make, as *deify, liquefy, solidify*
-hood, condition, as *fatherhood, falsehood*
-ic, pertaining to, as *historic, democratic*
-ice, act of, as *justice, police, practice*
-il, -ile, pertaining to, capable of being, as *civil, juvenile, mobile*
-ity, -ty, state or condition, as *sanity, acidity, safety*
-ious, full of, as *laborious, rebellious*
-ist, one who, as *pianist, machinist*
-ity, ty, state or condition, as *sanity, acidity, safety*
-ize, -yze, to make like, as *sympathize, analyze*
-less, without, as *careless, needless, hopeless*
-ly, manner, like, as *bodily, truthfully*
-ment, result, as *management, fragment*
-meter, measurement, as *thermometer, hydrometer*
-ness, state of being, as *sickness, happiness*

WORD PREFIXES, SUFFIXES AND ROOTS

-nomy, pertaining to laws or government, distribution, arrangement, as *economy, harmony, astronomy*

-ory, place where, as *directory, rectory*

-ous, -ious, -eous, -uous, full of, as *dangerous, melodious, beauteous, strenuous*

-ose, full of, as *morose, verbose*

-ship, state or quality, as *friendship, worship*

-some, like, full of, as *gruesome, tiresome*

-ster, one who, person doing something, as *gangster, songster*

-sion, -tion, act or state of being, as *conception, perception*

-tude, condition, as *fortitude, magnitude*

-ty, ity, condition, as *clarity, peculiarity, sanity*

-ule, little, as *globule, granule*

-ure, act of, as *departure, manufacture*

-ward, direction of course, as *backward, forward, downward*

-y, full of, characterized by, as *filthy, icy, soapy*

Latin and Greek Word Roots

Following are Latin and Greek word roots which are used in English words. Word roots give the word its basic meaning, whereas prefixes or suffixes modify or change the root word. The root word is given in bold face type followed by the meaning of the root. Examples of the roots are printed in italic type. Many word roots are generally used only as prefixes or suffixes. However, as you examine the examples, you will note that many appear at the beginning, in the middle, or at the end of the English word.

aero, air, as *aerodynamics, aerospace*

ag, ac, to do, as *agenda, action*

agr, agri, agro, farm, as *agriculture, agronomy*

anthropo, man, as *anthropology, anthropoid, misanthrope*

aqua, water, as *aqueous, aquatic*

arch, rule, principle, chief, as *archbishop, archenemy, anarchy*

astra, astro, star, as *astronomy, astral, astronomical*

aud, audi, audio, hearing, as *audience, auditor, audiovisual*

auto, self, oneself, as *automatic, autograph*

biblio, bib, book, as *bibliophile, Bible*

bio, life, as *biology, biosphere*

cad, cas, fall, as *cadence, cascade, casual*

cant, sing, as *cantata, chant*

cap, cep, take, as *captive, accept*

capit, head, as *capital, capitate*

cat, cath, down, through, as *cataract, catheter*

ced, cess, go, yield, as *procedure, cession, antecedent*

cide, cis, kill, cut, as *suicide, excise, incision*

clud, clus, close, as *include, inclusion, preclude*

cred, believe, as *creditor, creditable, creed*

dec, ten, as *decimal*

dem, people, as *democracy, demagogue*

dent, tooth, as *indent, dental*

derm, skin, as *dermatology, taxidermist*

dic, dict, say, speak, as *diction, dictate, predicate*

WORD PREFIXES, SUFFIXES AND ROOTS

duc, lead, as *induce, ductile*

equ, equal, as *equivalent, equitable, equality*

fac, fec, make, do, as *manufacture, infection*

fring, break as *infringement*

fract break as *fracture, fractious*

frater, brother, as *fraternal, fraternize*

fund, fus, pour as *refund, confuse*

gam, gamos marriage as *monogamous, bigamist, polygamous*

gen, produce as *generate, generation*

geo, earth as *geology, geometry, geography*

gastro, gast, stomach as *gastronomy, gastritis*

greg, group as *gregarious*

gress, grad walking, moving as *progress, degrade, retrograde*

gyn, woman as *gynecologist*

hemo, blood, as *hemorrhage, hemorroid*

homo, man, same as *homocide, homogeneous*

hydr, water as *dehydrate, hydralic*

idio, own, private, as *idiocy, idiosyncrasy*

iso, equal as *isothermal, isomorph*

ject, throw as *reject, project*

jud, jur, right as *judge, jury*

logy, study of as *psychology, biology*

loqu, speak as *loquacious, eloquent*

mand, order as *remand, command, demand*

manu, hand as *manuscript, manual*

mater, mother as *maternal, matricide*

meter, measure, as *thermometer, barometric*

micro, small as *microscopic, microbe*
mit, mis send as *permit, commission*
mono, mon, single, one as *monotony, monogram, monarch*
mort, death as *mortician, mortal*
nom, law as *economy, astronomy*
onym, name as *synonym, pseudonym*
pathos, feeling as *pathology, pathos*
philo, love as *philosophy, philosophical*
phobia, fear as *claustrophobia, hydrophobia*
porto, carry as *portable, export, report, transport*
pseudo, false as *pseudonym, pseudo*
psych, mind as *psychiatry, psychic, psychology*
scope, see as *telescope, microscope*
scrib, write as *inscription, description*
sec, cut as *dissect, bisect, resection*
sens, feel as *sensuous, sensitive*
sequ, follow as *sequence, inconsequent*
spec, spect, look as *specimen, inspect, spectacular*
spir, breath as *inspire, respiratory*
state, stand as *status, statutory*
ten, hold as *retention, detention*
term, end as *terminal, interminable*
typ, print as *typography, typewriter*
ven, vent, come as *prevent, convene, adventure*
vert, vers, turn as *divert, subversion, controversy*
vict, conquer as *evict, victim*
vid, vis, see as *video, visual, revise*
voc, call as *vocal, vocation*

Chapter 8

GUIDE FOR COMPOUNDING WORDS AND USE OF HYPHENS

A compound is two or more words joined together either with a hyphen or without a hyphen. Many words have become compound words through custom or usage because they are regularly used in succession or because the meaning is somewhat more clear or precise when the words are combined. The hyphen, when used in a compound word, is a mark of punctuation. Its purpose is to join the parts of a compound but also to separate the parts for better readability and clearer understanding. When in doubt about the compounding or hyphenation of a word, always consult your dictionary.

1. General Rule. Two or more words are not compounded unless the compounding aids understanding or readability. If the first word is principally an adjective describing the second word the words usually are not joined.

real estate	martial law	machine shop
book value	marble cake	fish hawk
tail wind	sun parlor	roller bearing

2. Nouns. Many nouns are formed by two other nouns

(including gerunds) and are written as one word either by repeated usage or because as one word they better express a single thought or idea.

redhead	northeast	eggplant
locksmith	raindrop	doorman
eyewitness	laughingstock	bathroom

3. Verb and Adverb Compounds. Verbs and adverbs are often joined together or with nouns to express a literal or nonliteral figurative thought.

viewpoint	striptease	outwork
upgrade	rearmost	pushover
troublesome	pennywise	breakdown

4. Compound Personal Pronouns. Write compound personal pronouns as one word.

myself	himself	ourself
yourself	herself	themselves

5. Any, Every, Some, No. When these words are combined with *body, thing* or *where*, they should be written as one word. When *one* is the second element, and the meaning is a single or particular person, group, or thing, write as two words. No *one* is always two words.

anybody	everywhere	nowhere
anything	somebody	nothing
everyone	something	no one

Everyone came. *but*: Every one of the boys came.

6. Compound Modifiers (Adjectives). When words or numerals are combined to modify a noun, they should be hyphenated when they precede the word modified. However, see the rules which follow.

long-term lease	two-time candidate
short-wave radio	reddish-brown color
2-volume set	single-engine plane

(a) Certain types of unit modifiers should not be hyphenated. A precise rule can not be given. However, in general the two modifying words are words that are regularly used together in other contexts, the first word is a modifier of the second word, and then the two words together serve to identify or describe the third word.

life insurance policy	high school student
special delivery mail	civil rights law
income tax return	real estate tax
atomic energy plant	social security law

(b) Omit the hyphen in a unit modifier when it follows the word modified.

The area is middle class.
   but: It is a middle-class area.
The company is well financed.
   but: It is a well-financed company.

(c) Omit the hyphen in a unit modifier if the first word is a comparative or superlative.

lower priced stock	low-priced stock
best developed plan	well-developed plan
highest salaried group	high-salary group

(d) Descriptive words are not hyphenated when one of the words is an adverb.

happily awaited event   suprisingly long time
socially accepted custom   lovely young girl

(e) If a series of two or more compounds has the same basic word and this word is omitted except as the last term, retain all the hyphens.

first-, second-, and third-class mail
part- or full-time work
4-, 5-, and 6-foot lumber

(f) Omit the hyphen in foreign phrases used as modifiers.

prima facie evidence   bona fide signature
per diem payment   ex officio chairman

7. **Miscellaneous Rules**.

(a) Compound words containing proper nouns and beginning with the prefixes *anti-*, *ex*, *pro*, and *un*, as well as those ending with the suffix *elect*, are hyphenated.

ex-President Carter   Senator-elect Harris
pro-British   un-American

(b) Use hyphens to connect capital letters to words forming adjectives or nouns.

an A-line skirt   a V-line blouse
an S-curve   a T-square

(c) Compound numbers over twenty and less than one hundred are hyphenated.

> twenty-one   one hundred eighty-six
> sixty-three   six hundred forty-two

(d) Two-word fractions are hyphenated only when they are used as adjectives. They are not hyphenated when functioning as nouns.

> A two-thirds majority voted in favor, (an adjective)
> Two thirds of the members voted in favor. (a noun)

(e) A range in numbers or in the alphabet is indicated by a hyphen.

> 10-31 (meaning 10 through 31)
> M-S   (meaning M through S)

(f) Compound nouns and adjectives with the prefix *self* are hyphenated.

> self-restraint (n)   self-induced (a)
> self-interest (n)   self-service (a)

Chapter 9

RULES FOR WORD DIVISION

1. Avoid dividing a word at the end of a line unless necessary to maintain good margins. Do not divide the last word in a paragraph or the last word on a page.

2. If it is necessary to divide, divide a word only between syllables; but even then, apply the following rules:

3. Do not separate a single letter syllable from the rest of the word.

> Right: emo-tion   Wrong: e-motion
> Right: abu-sive   Wrong: a-busive

4. Avoid dividing a word before or after a two letter syllable.

> Avoid: el-evate   Better: ele-vate
> Avoid: cavi-ty   Better: cav-ity

5. Do not divide words of five or fewer letters even if the word has more than one syllable.

> Wrong: In-dia, Indi-a   Correct: India
> Wrong: i-deal, ide-al   Correct: ideal

RULES FOR WORD DIVISION

6. Where the final consonant is doubled before a suffix, the added consonant goes with the suffix. However, if the root word ends with a double letter, divide after the double letter.

> Right: assess-ing   Wrong: asses-sing
> Right: allot-ted   Wrong: allotted

7. Words of one syllable should never be divided. Examples: whom, mend, passed, scrubbed.

Chapter 10

PUNCTUATION RULES

When you are writing, punctuation marks are signals from you to your reader. A period indicates that you have ended a sentence or that an abbreviation has been used. A comma may mean that there is a slight break in thought, indicate two separate parts of a compound sentence; or it may be used in one of several other ways.

Some sentences may be punctuated in more than one way; and, in some instances, a punctuation mark is a matter of choice by the writer. To help you punctuate expertly, the following rules and examples are given.

THE PERIOD (.)

1. Use a period at the end of a declarative or imperative sentence. (Also see Rule 5 under quotations.)

> The letter arrived this morning.   (declarative)
> Ship our order immediately. (imperative)

2. Use a period rather than a question mark after an indirect question or courteous request.

> He asked if you had received it yet.   (indirect question)

Will you please ship it today. (courteous request)

3. Use a period after abbreviations, initials, and contractions. Abbreviations do not have internal spacing.

Mr.   qt.   P.M.   etc.   U.S.A.

4. At the end of a sentence, a period is sufficient for both an abbreviation and the sentence.

Send it to McDonald and Son, Inc.

5. Use three periods (ellipis marks) to indicate the omission of words from a quotation.

"Democracy is the government of the people . . . for the people." --Abraham Lincoln

6. Use four periods when the omission comes at the end of a quoted passage.

"Get your facts first, and then you can distort them . . . ." --Mark Twain

Note: Do not use a period at the end of a title of a book, magazine article, poem, etc. unless the title ends a sentence. In typed material, there should be two spaces between a period ending a sentence and the beginning of the next sentence.

THE QUESTION MARK (?)

1. Use the question mark after all direct questions.

Did you receive the report?
Have you shipped our order yet?

2. In a sentence containing more than one question each separate query may use a question mark.

Are you certain of the place? the time? the date?

But if a question is not complete until the final word of the sentence, the question mark should be at the end only.

Do you want to meet me at two p.m., three p.m., or four p.m.?

3. The question mark may also be used when only part of the sentence is a question, and in such sentences, the question is often introduced by a comma or colon; a semicolon or dash is sometimes used.

Please tell me, why are you going?
We must analyze the problem: Have you any suggestions?
I have explained the problem: Have you any suggestions?

Note: In typed material, leave two spaces after the question mark and the beginning of the next sentence.

PUNCTUTATION RULES

THE EXCLAMATION MARK (!)

1. Use the exclamation mark after all exclamatory sentences which convey surprise, strong emotion, or deep feeling.

> I can't believe you failed to complete the job!
> What a lovely thing to do!

2. Use the exclamation mark after interjections or after statements which emphasize commands or which suggest immediate action.

> Please! Ship our order immediately.
> Act now! Don't wait!

3. Use the exclamation mark after an interrogative sentence that is intended to be exclamatory.

> Oh no, how can you tell him that!
> Isn't she too young to understand!

4. The exclamation mark is also used to add emphasis.

> Your deadline is midnight!
> This is your last chance!

Note: In typed material, use two spaces after an exclamation mark and before the beginning of the next sentence.

THE COMMA (,)

1. When a dependent clause precedes the main clause,

use the comma to separate the introductory clause. However, the comma is usually unnecessary when the dependent clause does not begin the sentence.

> When he completed his assignment, he went to see the dean. (comma)
> The chairman asked for the voting to begin after everyone was in the room. (no comma)

2. Use the comma after an absolute phrase or a participial phrase at the beginning of a sentence.

> The snow storm having begun, we decided to stay at home.
> Having completed the test in less than an hour, she left the room.

3. Use the comma after an introductory infinitive phrase. But do not separate the subject from the rest of the sentence when it is an infinitive.

> To be helpful, you must know when to offer help.
> To be helpful was her wish.

4. Use the comma to set off parenthetical elements in a sentence, such as words, phrases, clauses, or expressions. (Also see Rule 1 under parenthesis and Rule 1 under the dash.)

(a) Transitional words should be followed by commas

(*besides, consequently, however, moreover, therefore*).

However, I did not feel it was necessary.

Phrases, such as *in short, as a result, of course,* or *so to speak,* should be set off by commas.

As I wrote before, there is, of course, a way out.
As a result, our losses will be less than expected.

Use the comma to set off clauses (*I think, he says, we suppose*).

The president, I think, will be concerned.

Expressions should be set off by commas when the logical progression of words is interrupted (*so far as she is concerned,* and *I respect his view*).

The chairman did not object, and I respect his view, to staggering vacation time over a two-month period.

5. Introductory expressions are set off by commas (*indeed, yes, surely,* meaning *yes, well*).

Yes, I am going to attend.
Well, I would not have accepted the report.

6. A nonrestrictive clause is set off by a comma because it gives added information about the word it mod-

ifys, but it is not needed to complete sentence meaning.
A restrictive clause is needed to complete the meaning
of a sentence, and, therefore, is never set off by commas.

> The new manager, who is thirty-three, certainly is
> doing a good job. (The non-restrictive clause *who
> is thirty-three* gives added information but is not
> needed to complete the meaning of the sentence.)
> The new manager who came from sales is now in
> charge. (The restrictive clause *who came from
> sales* is necessary to identify the word *manager*.
> Therefore, no commas are used.)

7. Use a comma to separate a word in opposition that
defines or identifies another word with a noun.

> Mary, my secretary, is very efficient.
> My secretary, Mary, is very efficient.

8. Use a comma to separate words that indicate direct
address.

> Scott, please read the enclosed report.

9. Use a comma to separate a series of words, phrases,
or clauses.

> The recipe calls for, eggs, cream, and sugar.
> She ran down the street, into a driveway, back to

the curb, and sat down crying.

If we accept the proposal, it means that: (1) we will have three weeks vacation, (2) we will be paid for overtime, (3) we will have maternity leave.

10. Use the comma to separate coordinate adjectives which modify the same noun if the word *and* can be substituted for the comma.

The new, efficient machine will increase our production. (The new *and* efficient machine.)

The present operating plan will be changed. (No comma. You would not say present *and* operating.)

11. Use a comma before the conjunctions *and, but, for, or, nor,* and *yet* when they join the independent clauses of a compound sentence.

I sent the letter as you requested, and we should have a reply soon.

She asked for him on the telephone, but no one was there by that name.

(a) The comma may be omitted between most short clauses and between some long clauses when the meaing is clear.

He searched but did not find the report.

(b) When the comma is used without a coordinate conjunction between two independent clauses it is called the *comma fault*.

The children going to school do not cross at the intersection, they repeatedly jay-walk. (Incorrect -- a coordinate conjunction should be used after the comma.)

To eliminate the comma fault, the sentence may be punctuated in any one of the three following ways:

The children going to school do not cross at the intersection, and they repeatedly jay-walk. (using a coordinate conjunction)

The children going to school do not cross at the intersection; they repeatedly jay-walk. (using a semicolon)

The children going to school do not cross at the intersection. They repeatedly jay-walk. (using two simple sentences)

Use a semicolon before the coordinate conjunction when the independent clauses of a compound sentence are very long or contain internal punctuation.

The children going to school do not cross at the intersection; and, as a result, they repeatedly jay-walk.

12. Use the comma to separate words or phrases that express contrast.

The supervisor, not the foreman, offered to help.

13. Use the comma to set off a month, year or definite place.

> He was born December 3, 1954, at 1612 Fardale Road, Jenkintown, Pennsylvania.

14. Use the comma to set off a direct short quotation. (See rule 4 under Quotations.)

> The employer asked, "Where do you expect to be in the next five years?"

15. Use the comma to separate a declarative clause and an interrogative clause which follows it.

> Terry will receive the award, will she not?

16. Use the comma to set off a sentence element when it is out of its natural order or when it separates inverted names, or phrases.

> That she could accept the suggestion, none of us seriously doubted.
> Buckley, William S.
> Like you, I feel the time is not right.

17. Use a comma to indicate the omission of a word.

> Mark is extremely sensitive to the feelings of others; Scott, totally indifferent. (The word *is* has been omitted.)

18. Use the comma to separate a proper name from an academic degree or honorary title. Also use a comma between two or more degrees or titles.

> Mary Jones, B.S.N., M.S., F.A.A.N., Director of Nursing.

19. Use a comma to separate the thousands in figures of four digits or more.

> 1,200   22,200   3,000,000

20. Use a comma to separate two sets of figures or two identical words.

> Bring me 5, No. 1040, and 10, No. 1140.
> Where he is, is not known.

Note: In typed material, use one space after a comma.

THE SEMICOLON (;)

The semicolon (;) indicates a more complete separation between sentence elements than does the comma. Overuse of the semicolon should be avoided.

1. Use the semicolon to separate independent coordinate clauses that are related in meaning when no coordinate conjunction is used. (Rule 11 under Comma.)

> The staff members desired a change in direction; they were eager to offer suggestions.

PUNCTUTATION RULES

2. Use the semicolon between coordinate clauses of a compound sentence when they are united by transitional words.

> The freeholders approved the building plans; as a result, construction will resume next spring.

Commonly used transitional words:

accordingly	furthermore	nevertheless
as a result	however	otherwise
besides	in addition	that is
consequently	indeed	therefore
finally	in fact	thus
for example	moreover	yet
for this reason	namely	

3. Use the semicolon before a coordinate conjunction (*and, but, for, or, nor*) to separate two independent clauses with internal punctuation. (Rule 11 under Commas.)

> The meeting, which ran overtime, was boring; but some decisions were made in spite of weak presentations.

4. Use the semicolon before words such as *for example, for instance, namely,* or *that is* which introduce an example, enumeration, or items in a series.

> The committee was represented by four officers; namely, the president, vice-president, secretary, and treasurer.

5. Use the semicolon in clarifying listings where a comma is insufficient to separate the items clearly.

> Committee members who attended were James Farley, president; Timothy Sullivan, vice-president; and Jean Shelley, secretary.

Note: In typed material use one space after a semi-colon.

THE COLON (:)

1. Use the colon before a list of items or enumerations.

> See if we have the following merchandise in stock: No. 42, No. 63, and No. 67.
> My itinerary included: going on a bus trip, visiting several museums, and shopping for jewelery.

(a) When the list of items is in a column, capitalize the first letter.

> You must hire someone who has technical skills in the following areas:
>   1. Computer programming
>   2. Audio/Video camera
>   3. Software production

(b) When the items are presented in a sentence it is not necessary to capitalize the first letter.

You must hire someone who has technical skills in the following areas: computer programming, audio/visual camera, and software production.

2. Use the colon before an appositive phrase.

The jury rules were simply stated: no radio, no television, no visitors.

3. Use the colon following the salutation of a business letter.

Dear Mr. Greene: Gentlemen:

Do not use a semicolon after a salutation. However, a comma may be used after the salutation of an informal letter.

Dear Kathy,   Dear Mother,

4. Use the colon to divide the parts of formulas, numbers, references, or titles.

The conferences will begin at 10:30 A.M.
The pastor quoted from Chapter VI: Page 10.

PARENTHESES ( )

1. Use parentheses to separate words, phrases, clauses, or sentences which enclose material that explains, translates or comments. (Rule 4 under commas. Rule 1 under the dash.)

She swam 1500 meters (somewhat less than a mile).
He stated, "E pluribus unum." (One out of many.)

2. Use parentheses to enclose letters, numbers, or symbols when referring to an appositive.

We made reservations for fifteen (15) days.

(a) Use parentheses with other punctuation marks. If the punctuation mark is connected to the entire sentence and not just to the parenthetical part, the punctuation mark follows the second parenthesis.

They carefully analyzed and evaluated the standards (legal and moral), but could not reach a decision.

(b) The punctuation mark should be placed within the second parenthesis if it applies only to material concerning the parenthetical section.

You may save a life by giving first-aid to someone who is choking. (See the back cover of this pamphlet.)

THE DASH (—)

The dash should be used to indicate a sudden change of ideas, but should be used sparingly. The dash may be used for emphasis or for visual effect.

PUNCTUTATION RULES

1. Use the dash to indicate an abrupt change of thought in a sentence or strong parenthetical expressions.

> She feels — how can I say that? — like an outcast.
> I was annoyed — no, shocked to be more specific — by his behavior.

2. Use the dash to set off a summary or an afterthought that is added to a sentence.

> The educational team will make an evaluation and draw up a plan — in fact, they will provide a complete special program for the child.

3. Use the dash to emphasize a word or phrase that is repeated.

> The president stated that we had one week — one week only — to make a decision.

4. Use a dash to mark limits between dates, numbers, places, and times.

> The admissions office is open 9:00 — 4:30 daily.
> Read pages 22-40.

THE QUOTATION MARK (" ")

1. Use quotation marks to enclose all direct quotations.

> "Yes," she said, "I did help to raise funds."

The teacher asked if she gave you the date for the test.

2. Use quotation marks to enclose the chapters of a book, names of songs, titles of magazine articles or poems, and other similar titles. In typing or writing, underline titles of books, magazines, operas, and any other work long enough to appear in book form. Underlining of titles signifies italics for printing.

The National Geographic includes a section called "Members Forum."

"The Owl and the Pussy Cat" is a child's favorite poem.

3. Use quotation marks to set off words, phrases, or sentences referred to within a sentence or to emphasize a word. (Italics may also be used in such cases.)

The sentence "you can't take it with you" has deep meaning for some people.

The word "judgement" is often misspelled.

What was the real "meaning" of his asking?

PUNCTUTATION RULES

4. Use quotation marks at the beginning of each paragraph if several paragraphs are quoted, and at the end of the last paragraph. Very long quotations are frequently introduced by a colon instead of a comma. (Rule 14 under commas.) Usually indent quotations of three or more lines from the body.

5. Using quotation marks with other punctuation:

(a) Place a period or comma before ending quotation marks.

> She said, "No one is home."
> "No one is home," she said.

(b) Place the question mark before quotation marks when they refer to the quoted content, or after when they refer to the complete sentence.

> He said, "Why do you want to see her"?
> Did he say, "Why do you want to see her?"

(c) Place the semicolon and colon after ending quotation marks unless they are part of the quoted material.

> He said, "You are to be our next president"; therefore, I hope you you will consider me for your present job.

Chapter 11

RULES OF CAPITALIZATION

1. Capitalize the first word of a sentence.

Your order has been shipped.

2. Capitalize the first word of a line of poetry.

"Poems are made by fools like me...."

3. Capitalize the first word of a direct quotation.

He asked, "Where are the parts?"

4. Capitalize *proper nouns* (names of specific persons, places, or things).

New York City	Henry Jones	Wall Street
Lake Michigan	Brazil	Holiday Inn

5. Capitalize *proper adjectives* (adjectives formed from proper nouns).

American	Spanish	Southern
Communistic	Chinese	Russian

6. Capitalize names of *specific organizations* or *institutions*.

Northwestern University	Republican Party
American Red Cross	Ford Motor Company

RULES OF CAPITALIZATION

7. Capitalize *days of the week, months of the year, holidays,* and *days of special observance.*

Sunday	August	Yom Kippur
Mother's Day	Easter	Christmas
Feast of the Passover	St. Valentines Day	

8. Capitalize *names of the seasons* only if they are personified.

Personified	*Season*
Springs warm touch	spring breezes
Winter's icy breath	winter's snow

9. Always capitalize *languages* but not other school subjects unless they are names of specific courses.

English	Chemistry 101	but: chemistry
French	Economics 102	economics
Spanish	Composition 200	composition

10. Capitalize *races, religions,* and *ethnic groups.*

Negro	Catholic	Moslem
Eurasian	Presbyterian	Japanese

11. Capitalize references to the *Diety* and to the *titles of holy books.*

God, the Father	the Trinity	the Koran
Supreme Being	Genesis	Talmud

12. Capitalize *titles of people* when they are followed by a name.

119

President Henderson   Senator Hutchins
Cardinal Wilson   Professor Stark
Doctor Allison   Reverend Harmon

13. Capitalize sections of a *country*, but do not capitalize directions.

Sections	*Directions*
the Midwest	I traveled west.
the Near East	The sun rose in the east.
the South	They went south.

14. Capitalize titles of *works of literature, art,* and *music*. However, in such titles do not capitalize short prepositions, articles, and conjunctions unless they are the first word.

War and Peace   Battle Hymn of the Republic
The Angelus   Beethoven's Fifth Symphony
Book of Job   The Last of the Mohicans

15. Capitalize *names of governmental bodies* and *departments*.

President's Cabinet   Civil Service Commission
Supreme Court   Bureau of the Census
United States Senate   the Federal Government

16. Capitalize *words which show family relationships* when they are used with a person's name or when they stand unmodified as a substitute for a person's name.

Aunt Alyce   my aunt
Grandfather Scott   his grandfather

I sent a package to Mother. (but: My mother will be there.)

RULES OF CAPITALIZATION

17. Capitalize names of *definite regions, localities*, and *political divisions*.

the Orient	Fourth Precinct
the Artic Circle	First Ward (of a city)
French Republic	Bergen County

18. Capitalize names of *historical events, historical periods* and *historical documents*.

the Middle Ages	Magna Carta
World War II	the Crusades
Bill of Rights	Third Amendment

19. The names of separate departments of a business may be written with either capital or small letters. Business titles such as president, office manager, superintendent, etc. may be written either way.

The Company will pay your expenses.
 (or company)
Our President will see you June 6.
 (or president)
Research Department *or* research department.

20. The pronoun *I* should always be capitalized.

It is I who will go.

Chapter 12

RULES FOR ABBREVIATIONS

Rules for the use of abbreviations that apply to all situations cannot be given. In general, abbreviations should be avoided in business letters and other formal writing except as stated in the rules given below.

1. Use abbreviations for the courtesy titles *Mr. Mrs. Ms.* and *Dr.* These are never spelled out.

2. Abbreviations for titles of college faculty, military, personnel, government officials, clergy. etc. may be used if followed by a full name (first name and surname). If only the surname is used, the title should be written out.

Prof. Carl Harris Sr. *but*: Professor Harris (Never use Professor Harris Sr. Use Sr. or Jr. only with the full names.)

Rev. Thomas Kean *but*: The Reverend Dr. *or* Mr. *or* Father Kean (never Reverend Kean).

Gov. Ralph Peters *but*: Governor Peters

Hon. Ralph Peters *but*: The Honorable Ralph Peters *or* The Honorable Mr. Peters

Adm. Scott Risner *but*: Admiral Risner

RULES FOR ABBREVIATIONS

3. Academic degrees should be abbreviated after a full name.

Henry Munoz, Ph.D. *or* Doctor or Professor Munoz
Ray Albitz, M.D. *or* Dr. Ray Albitz or Doctor Albitz *never* Doctor or Dr. Ray Albitz, M.D.

4. Abbreviate the names of organizations without periods when the full names are widely known.

AFL-CIO	UNESCO
DAR	NAACP
AT&T	ITT

5. Abbreviate the names of government agencies and military services and terms when they are widely known. They are usually written without periods.

USN	GAO	FBI
USAF	HEW	NATO
PX	CIA	SEC

6. Geographic abbreviations composed of initials require periods after each initial but no internal spacing. (When *United States, United Kingdom,* etc. are used as nouns they should not be abbreviated.)

U.S.A.	U.A.R.
U.K.	U.S.S.R.

7. Widely known business terms may be abbreviated

followed by periods or they may be in all capitals with
no periods.

F.O.B. or FOB or f.o.b.	(free on board)
C.O.D. or COD or c.o.d.	(collect on delivery)
E.O.M. or EOM or e.o.m.	(end of month)

8. In business letters and other formal writing do not
abbreviate the names of days of the week, cities, states,
countries (except widely known abbreviations such as
U.S. and U.S.S.R.), weights and measures, or the words
street and *avenue*. Exception: If in a business letter there
is a listing of several items accompanied by figures such
as 23 *lbs.*, it may be acceptable to use abbreviations
depending somewhat on the purpose of the listing, its
length, appearance, etc. In invoices, tables, and statistical
work such abbreviations, including days of the week,
etc., would normally be used and usually without periods.

9. Abbreviate certain foreign terms in frequent use.

etc.   e.g.   i.e.

Chapter 13

LIST OF ABBREVIATIONS
STATES AND TERRITORIES

	ZIP 2-Letter	Regular		ZIP 2-Letter	Regular
Alabama	AL	Ala.	Missouri	MO	Mo.
Alaska	AK	*Alas.	Montana	MT	Mont.
Arizona	AZ	Ariz.	Nebraska	NE	Nebr.
Arkansas	AR	Ark.	Nevada	NV	Nev.
California	CA	Calif.	New Hampshire	NH	N.H.
Canal Zone	CZ	C.Z.	New Jersey	NJ	N.J.
Colorado	CO	Colo.	New Mexico	NM	N. Mex.
Connecticut	CT	Conn.	New York	NY	N.Y.
Delaware	DE	Del.	North Carolina	NC	N.C.
District of			North Dakota	ND	N. Dak.
Columbia	DC	D.C.	Ohio	OH	*O.
Florida	FL	Fla.	Oklahoma	OK	Okla.
Georgia	GA	Ga.	Oregon	OR	Ore.
Guam	GU	**	Pennsylvania	PA	Penna.
Hawaii	HI	**	Puerto Rico	PR	P.R.
Idaho	ID	*Ida.	Rhode Island	RI	R.I.
Illinois	IL	Ill.	South Carolina	SC	S.C.
Indiana	IN	Ind.	South Dakota	SD	S. Dak.
Iowa	IA	*Ia.	Tennessee	TN	Tenn.
Kansas	KS	Kans.	Texas	TX	*Tex.
Kentucky	KY	Ky.	Utah	UT	**
Louisiana	LA	La.	Vermont	VT	Vt.
Maine	ME	*Me.	Virginia	VA	Va.
Maryland	MD	Md.	Virgin Islands	VI	V.I.
Massachusetts	MA	Mass.	Washington	WA	Wash.
Michigan	MI	Mich.	West Virginia	WV	W. Va.
Minnesota	MN	Minn.	Wisconsin	WI	Wis.
Mississippi	MS	Miss.	Wyoming	WY	Wyo.

* Avoid abbreviating   ** No regular abbreviation

Note: The 2-letter abbreviation without periods should be used with zip codes.

LIST OF ABBREVIATIONS
CANADIAN PROVINCES

Alberta	AB	Nova Scotia	NS
British Columbia	BC	Ontario	ON
Labrador	LB	Prince Edward	
		Island	PE
Manitoba	MB	Quebec	PQ
New Brunswick	NB	Saskatchewan	SK
Newfoundland	NF	Yukon Territory	YT
Northwest	NT		
Territories			

MONTHS OF THE YEAR

January	Jan.	July	*Jul. or Jy.
February	Feb.	August	Aug.
March	Mar.	September	Sep. or Sept.
April	Apr.	October	Oct.
May	*My.	November	Nov.
June	*Jun. or Je.	December	Dec.

* Avoid abbreviating

DAYS OF THE WEEK

Sunday	Sun. or S.	Thursday	Thurs. or Th.
Monday	Mon. or M.	Friday	Fri. or F.
Tuesday	Tues. or Tu.	Saturday	Sat. or Sa.
Wednesday	Wed. or W.		

Avoid use of the short abbreviation

126

LIST OF ABBREVIATIONS

U.S. MILITARY ABBREVIATIONS

AAF, Army airfield
Adj, Adjt, adjutant

ADM, Admiral;
Admiralty
AFB, air force base
AIC, airman, first
class
AG, Adjutant
General
AHQ, Army
headquarters
AMG, Allied
Military
Government
ANC, Army Nurse
Corps
APO, Army Post
Office
AR, Army regulation
ASN, Army service
number
AUS, Army of the
United States
AWOL, absent
without leave

BG, Brigadier
General

CAPT, Captain,
(Navy)
CDR, Commander,

(Navy)
CG, Coast Guard;
Commanding
General
CH, Chaplain
CINC, Commander
in Chief
CMC, Commandant
of the Marine Corps
Cmdr, Commander,
(Army)
CO, Commanding
Officer
COL, Colonel
Comdt,
Commandant
CPL, corporal
CPO, chief petty
officer
CPT, Captain
(Army)
CWO, Chief
Warrant Officer
CW2, Chief Warrant
Officer, W-2

DA, Department of
the Army
DAV, Disabled
American Veterans
DD, dishonorable
discharge
DN, Department of

the Navy
DOD, Department of
Defense

ENS, Ensign

FLT, First
Lieutenant
FSg, first sergeant
FAdm, Fleet
Admiral
FPO, Fleet Post
Office

GA, General of the
Army
GCM, general court
martial
GEN, General
GFI, Government
free issue
GHQ, general
headquarters
GI, general issue;
Government issue;
member of U.S.
armed forces

HD, honorable
discharge
HG, headquarters

IG, Inspector
General
inf, infantry

JAG, Judge
Advocate General

KIA, killed in action

LCdr, Lieutenant
Commander
LCI, landing craft
infantry
LT, Lieutenant
LTC, Lieutenant
Colonel
LTjg, Lieutenant
(junior grade)

MAJ, Major
MATS, Military Air
Transport Service
MC, Marine Corps
MG, Major General
MI, Military
Intelligence
mil, military
MOS, military
occupational
speciality
MP, military police
MSG, master
sergeant

nav, naval; navigate
NC, Nurse Corps
NCO,
noncommissioned
officer

LIST OF ABBREVIATIONS

NG, National Guard
NR, Navy regulation

OCS, officer candidate school
OD, officer of the day
OG, officer of the guard
ONI, Office of Naval Intelligence
OPNAV, Office of the Chief of Naval Operations
OSA, Office of the Secretary of the Army
OSD, Office of the Secretary of Defense

PFC, private, first class
PG, permanent grade
PM, Provost Marshal
PO, petty officer
POW, PW, prisoner of war
PSG, platoon sergeant
PVT, private
PX, post exchange

QM, quartermaster

RAdm, Rear Admiral
ROTC, Reserve Officers' Training Corps
RG, reserve grade

S1c, seaman, first class
2LT, Second Lieutenant
SECDEF, Secretary of Defense
SECNAV, Secretary of the Navy
SFC, sergeant, first class
SGT, sergeant
SL, squad leader
SN, service number
SP, shore patrol; shore police
Sp4, specialist 4
SPAR, Coast Guard Women's Reserve
SR, service record
SSG, staff sergeant
SSS, Selective Service System
SG, Surgeon General

Ufo, Unidentified flying object
USA, U.S. Army
U.S.A., United

States of America
USAF, U.S. Air Force; U.S. Armed Forces
U.S.A.R., United States Army Reserve
USCG, U.S. Coast Guard
USGLI, U.S. Government Life Insurance
U.S.M.A., United States Military Academy
USMC, U.S. Marine Corps
U.S.N.G., United States National Guard
USN, U.S. Navy
USNR, U.S. Naval Reserve
U.S.S., United States Senate; United States ship

VAdm, Vice Admiral

WAC, Women's Army Corps; a Wac
W.A.A.C., Women's Army Auxiliary Corps
WAF, Women in the Air Force; a Waf
WAVES, women accepted for volunteer emergency service; women in the U.S. Navy; a Wave
WO, warrant officer

GENERAL ABBREVIATIONS

a, acre; alto; ampere; adjective; artillery
A., Absolute (temperature); angstrom unit; acre; American
AA, antiaircraft; Alcoholics Anonymous; Associate in Arts
AAA, antiaircraft artillery; Automobile Association of America
AAAS, American Association for the Advancement of Science
AARP, American Association for Retired Persons
A.B., B.A., Bachelor of Arts
ABA, American Bankers Association; American Bar Association
abbr., abbrev., abbreviated; -tion
ABC, atomic, biological, and chemical; Audit Bureau of Circulation; American Broadcasting Company; American Bowling Congress
ABM, antiballistic missile

LIST OF ABBREVIATIONS

abr., abridged; abridgment
abs., absolute; abstract; absent
ABS, American Bible Society
abst., abstr., abstract; abstracted
abt., about
AC, ac, alternating current; author's change
A/C, a/c, a., acct., account
acad., academic; academy
acct., account
accts. pay., AP, accounts payable
accts. rec., AR, accounts receivable
ack., ackgt., acknowledgment
ACLU, American Civil Liberties Union
ACP, American College of Physicians
ACS, American Chemical Society; American Cancer Society
ACTH, adrenocorticotropic hormone
acpt., acceptance
a.d., after date; average deviation
A.D. (anno Domini), in the year of our Lord
ADA, American Dental Association
ADC, Aid to Dependent Children
ad inf., (ad infinitum), to infinity
adj., adjective; adjourned; adjunct; adjustment; adjacent
ad lib. (ad libitum), as one wishes; as indicated

ad loc. (ad locum), to, or at, the place
adm., administrative; admitted
adm., admr., administrator
adv., advt., ad, advertising
adv., adverb; advice
ad val. (ad valorem), according to value
A.E., Agricultural Engineer; Aeronautical Engineer
A.E.A., Actor's Equity Association
AEC, Atomic Energy Commission
AESC, American Engineering Standards Committee
afft., affidavit
AF, af, audio frequency
AFL-CIO, American Federation of Labor and Congress of Industrial Organizations
AFM, American Federation of Musicians
AFTRA, American Federation of Television and Radio Artists
A.G., Adjutant General; Accountant General; Attorney General
agcy., agency
agr., agric., agricultural; agriculture
agt., agent; agreement
a-h, amp-hr, ampere-hour
A.H.A., American Hospital Association; American Historical Association

AIB, American Institute of Banking

AID, Agency for International Development

AKC, American Kennel Club

Al, alum., aluminum; aluminium

ALA, American Library Association

Ald., Aldm., Alderman

ALR, American Law Reports

alt., alternate; alternating; altitude; alto

Am., am., ammeter

Am., Amer., America; American

AM, amplitude modulation

A.M. (anno mundi), in the year of the world

A.M., a.m. ante meridiem), before noon

A.M., M.A., Master of Arts

AMA, American Medical Association; American Management Association

Amb., Ambassador

Amer., America; American

amdt., amendment

AMG, Allied Military Government

amp, amperage; ampere

amp-hr, a-h, ampere-hour

amt., amount

AMVETS, American Veterans of World War II

anal., analogous; analogy; analysis; analytic

analyt., analytical

anat., anatomy; -ical; -ist

antilog, antilogarithm

ann., annals; annual; annuity

annot., annotated; annotator

anon., anonymous

ans., answer; answered

anti., antiq., antiquarian; -quities

ant., antonym

anthrop., anthropol., anthropological; anthropology

AOA, American Osteopathic Assn.

AP, Associated Press

AP, A/P, ap, accounts payable

Ap., apothecaries

APA, American Pharmaceutical Association; American Psychological Association; American Psychiatric Association

app., apps., appendix; appendixes

App. Div., Appellate Division

approx., approximate; approximately

appt., appoint; appointment

appx., apx., appendix

apt., apartment

AR, A/R, ar, accounts receivable

ARC, American Red Cross

arch., archit., architect; architectural

archeol., archeology

arith., arithmetic; arithmetical

arr., arranged; -ments; arrival

ASA, American Statistical Association; American Standards

LIST OF ABBREVIATIONS

Association
ASAP, as soon as possible
ASCAP, American Society of Composers, Authors, and Publishers
ASCE, American Society of Civil Engineers
assd., assigned; assessed; assured
ASME, American Society of Mechanical Engineers
assn., ass'n, association
assoc., associate; association
asst., assistant
ATC, air traffic control
Atl., Atlantic
A.s.t., Atlantic standard time
astron., astronomer; astronomy
atm. press., atmosphere pressure
att., atty., attorney at law; attention
attn., attention
at. no., atomic number
at. vol., atomic volume
at. wt., atomic weight
aug., augmented; augmentative
auth., author; authentic; authorized
auto., automatic; automotive
aux., auxiliary
av., average; avoirdupois
Av., Ave., Avenue
advp., avoir., avoirdupois
avg., average
AWOL, absent without leave

b, born; book; brother; bass
BA, Bachelor of Arts

BAA, Bachelor of Applied Arts
B/B, bank balance
bal., balance
bar., barometer; barometric
BAS, Bachelor of Agricultural Sciences
bbl, barrel
BBT, basal body temperature
B.C., before Christ
BCG (bacillus Calmette-Guérin), antituberculosis vaccine
bd., band; board; bond; bound
bd. ft., board foot
bdl., bundle
BE, B/E, be, bill of exchange
BEC, Bureau of Employees' Compensation
BEV, bev, billion electron volts
BFA, Bachelor of Fine Arts
bf, boldface
bg, bag; background
bhp, brake horsepower
Bib., Bible; Biblical
bibliog., bibliography; -er; -ical
b.i.d. (*bis in die*), twice a day
biog., biography; -er; -ical
biol., biology; -ical; -ist
bk., bank; block; book
bkg., banking
BL, B/L, bl, bill of lading
bldg., building
B.Litt., Litt.B., Bachelor of Literature
blk., black; block
BLS, Bureau of Labor Statistics

Blvd., Boulevard
bm, board measure
BMR, basal metabolic rate
bo, buyer's option; back order
B.Mus., Bachelor of Music
bot., botany; -ical; -ist
bp, boiling point
BP, blood pressure
bpd, barrels per day
bpl, birthplace
Bros., Brothers
B.S., B. Sc., Bachelor of Science
BSHA, Bachelor of Science in Hospital Administration
BS, B/S, bs, bill of sale
BSN, Bachelor of Science in Nursing
Btu, British thermal units
bty, battery
bu, bushel
bur., bureau
bull., bulletin
Bus. Mgr., Business Manager
bv, book value
BW, biological warfare; bacteriological warfare
bx, box

c, curie; cycle; circa
c., ct., cent; carat
C., Celsius (centigrade)
C., Centigrade; hundred; calorie
©, copyright
ca. (circa), about; centare; cathode
CA, cronological age
CAA, Civil Aeronautics Administration
CAF, caf, cost and freight
cal., calories
c and sc, capitals and small capitals (letters)
can., canceled; cannon; canto
cap., capital
CAP, Civil Air Patrol
CARE, Cooperative for American Remittances to Europe
cat., catalog
cbd, cash before delivery
CBS, Columbia Broadcasting System
cc, cubic centimeter; chapters
CC, C/C, cc, carbon copy
CCA, Circuit Court of Appeals
CCC, Commodity Credit Corporation
C. Cls., Court of Claims
CCPA, Court of Customs and Patent Appeals
CCR, Commission on Civil Rights
C.D., Civil Defense
C/D, certificate of deposit
cd-ft, cord-foot
CE, Civil Engineer; Chemical Engineer
CEA, Council of Economic Advisers
CED, Committee for Economic Development
cent., centigrade; century; central
cert., certificate; certify
cf., compare
CFI, cfi, cost, freight, and

134

LIST OF ABBREVIATIONS

insurance

cfm, cubic feet per minute

cfs, cubic feet per second

cg, centigram; center of gravity

CGS, cgs, centimeter-gram-second

c-h, candle-hour

ch., chap., chapter

chem., chemical; chemist; chemistry

chg., change; charge

chgd., charged

chf., chief

chm., chmn., chairman

CIA, Central Intelligence Agency

CIF, cif, cost, insurance, and freight

circ., circuit; circumference

cit., citation; cited; citizen

C.J. (corpus juris), body of law; Chief Justice

ck., cask; check

cl, carload; centiliter; clause

CLI, cost of living index

CLU, Chartered Life Underwriter

cm, centimeter; circular mil (wire measure)

cml., coml., commercial

CNS, central nervous system

C/O, c/o, care of; carried over

Co., Company; County

COD, cod, cash on delivery

col., column; colonel

com.; comm., commentary; commerce; commission; committee; commonwealth

cons., consolidated; consonant;

consul

cont., con'd, continued

contr., contract; control; contrary; contralto

conv., convalescent; convenient; convention

co-op., co-operative

cop., ©, copyright

cor., corner; correction; corpus; correlative

Corp., Corporation; corporal

cos, cosine

cosec, cosecant

cosh, hyperbolic cosine

cot, cotangent

coth, hyperbolic cotangent

cp, chemically pure; candlepower

CPA, Certified Public Accountant

CPI, Consumer Price Index

cpm, cycles per minute

CPR, cardiopulmonary resuscitation

cps, cycles per second

cr., credit; creditor; circular; center

crit., critical; criticism

cs., case; cases; census

CSC, Civil Service Commission

CSS, Commodity Stabilization Service

c.s.t., central standard time

ct., court; cent

c.t., central time

ctn., carton; cotangent

ctr., center

cu-ft, cubic foot (feet)

cu-in, cubic inch

cur., current; currency
CWO, cwo, cash with order
cwt, hundredweight
cyc., cycle
cyl., cylinder

d, daughter; died; date
da., day; days
DA, district attorney
DAR, Daughters of the American Revolution
dB, db, decibel
dba, doing business as
dc, DC, direct current; Doctor of Chiropractic; (da capa) repeat from the beginning
d.d., days after delivery; delayed delivery
D.D., Doctor of Divinity
DCN, design change notice
dd., delivered
D.D.S., Doctor of Dental Surgery
deb., deben., debenture
dec., deceased; decrescendo; decrease
def., defendant; deferred; defined
del., delegate; deliver
diff., difference; differential
Dem., Democrat; Democratic
dept., dep't, department
der., deriv., derived; derivation
dft., defendant; draft
dg, decigram
dia., diam., diameter
diag., diagram
dict., dictionary; dictation
diff., difference; differential
dim., diminutive
dioc., diocese
dir., director; direction

disc., discount; discovered
disp., dispatch; dispensary
dist., distance; distinguish; district
Dist. Ct., District Court
div., divided; dividend; division; divorced
dkg, dekagram
dkl, dekaliter
dkm, dekameter
dl, deciliter
D. Litt., Doctor of Letters
dm, decimeter
DNA, deoxyribonucleic acid
do., (ditto), the same
D.O., Doctor of Osteopathy
DOA, dead on arrival
doc., document
dol., dollar
dom., domestic; dominion
doz, dozen
D.P.H., Doctor of Public Health
D.P.Hy., Doctor of Public Hygiene
dr., debit; debtor; dram; drachma
Dr., Doctor; Drive (street)
d.s.t., daylight saving time
dup., duplicate
D.V.M., Doctor of Veterinary Medicine
DWT, deadweight tons

E, east; eastern
e, erg
ea., each
ECG, EKG, electrocardiogram
econ., economic; economics
Ecosoc, Economic and Social Council
ECT, electroconvulsive therapy
Ed.D., Doctor of Education
edit., edited; editor; edition

LIST OF ABBREVIATIONS

e.d.t., eastern daylight time
ee, errors excepted
EEG, electroencephalogram
e.g. (exempli gratia), for example
EHF, extremely high frequency
emf, electromotive force
enc., encl., enclosure
ency., encyclopedia
engr., engineer; engraved
eom, end of month
ERP, European recovery program
esp., especially
Esq., Esqr., Esquire
est., estate; established; estimated
e.s.t., eastern standard time
estab., established
esu, electrostatic unit
e.t., eastern time
et al. (et alii), and others
etc. (et cetera), and so forth
et seq. (et sequens), and the following
ex., example; exchange
exch., exchange
exec., executor; executive
ex lib. (ex libris), from the books o
exp., expenses; export; express
ext., extended; extension; exterior; external

F, Fahr., Fahrenheit
f, farad; feminine; feet; foot
f., and following page; **ff.**, pages
f., fol., folio; following
FAA, Federal Aviation Agency
fac., factor; factory
fam., family; familiar
fas, free alongside ship
FBI, Federal Bureau of Investigation

FCC, Federal Communications Commission
FDA, Food and Drug Administration
FDIC, Federal Deposit Insurance Corporation
Fed., Federal
fem., f., feminine
FHA, Federal Housing Administration
fict., fiction
fig., figurative; figure
fl., flange; flash; fluid
fl dr., fluid dram
FM, frequency modulation
FMB, Federal Maritime Board
FMCS, Federal Mediation and Conciliation Service
FNMA, Federal National Mortgage Association (Fannie Mae)
fn, footnote
F.O., foreign office
FOB, fob, free on board
fol., folio; following
foll., following
FPC, Federal Power Commision
FPHA, Federal Public Housing Authority
fpm, feet per minute
fps, feet per second; frames per second
Fr., Father; franc; France; French
FR, Federal Register; full rate
FRS, Federal Reserve System
FSA, Federal Security Agency
FSLIC, Federal Savings & Loan Insurance Corporation
F. Supp., Federal Supplement
frt., freight
ft, feet; foot; fort

ft bm, fbm, feet board measure
ft-c, foot-candle
FTC, Federal Trade Commission
ft-l, foot-lambert
ft-lb, foot-pound
furl., furlough
fut., future; futures
fwd., forward
FWD, four-wheel drive

G, g, gauge; gold; grain; gram; gravity; gender
gal, gallon
GAO, General Accounting Office
GAR, Grand Army of the Republic
GAW, guaranteed annual wage
GCA, ground control approach
g.c.d., greatest common divisor
GCI, ground control intercept
g.c.m., greatest common measure
G.c.t., Greenwich civil time
gdn., guardian
gen., gender; general; genus
geog., geography; -er; geographical
geol., geology; -ist; -ical
geom., geometry; -ical
GFA, General Freight Agent
GI, general issue; Government issue
Gm, gm, gram
G.M., General Manager; Grand Master; guided missile
G.m.t., Greenwich mean time
GNP, gross national product
GOP, Grand Old Party; Republican Party
Gov., Governor
Govt., Government
GPA, General Passenger Agent
GPO, General Post Office; Government Printing Office

gpm, gallons per minute
gps, gallons per second
gr, grade; grain; gram; grammar; gross
grad., gradient; graduate; graduated
gr-wt, gross weight
GSA, General Services Administration; Girl Scouts of America
guar., guaranteed
gutt., drops

h, henry, height; harbor; husband
ha, hectare
H.C., House of Commons
hcf, highest common factor
hdkf., handkerchief
hdqrs., headquarters
hdwe., hardware
HE, high explosive; His Excellency; His Eminence
HEW, Department of Health, Education, and Welfare
hf, half
HF, high frequency
hg, hectogram; heliogram
HHFA, Housing and Home Finance Agency
hist., historical; history; historian; histology
hl, hectoliter
H.L., House of Lords
hm, hectometer
Hon., Honorable
hosp., hospital
hp, horsepower
hr, hour
H.R. House of Representatives
ht, hgt, height
hwm, high water mark

LIST OF ABBREVIATIONS

HV, high voltage
hwy., highway
hyp., hypoth., hypothesis
Hz, Hertz (cycles per second)

I., Is., Island; isle
IAEC, International Atomic Energy
 Commission
ibid. (ibidem), in the same place
ICC, Interstate Commerce
 Commission
id. (idem), the same
ID, inside diameter; inside
 dimensions; identification (card)
i.e. (id est), that is
IEEE, Institute of Electrical &
 Electronic Engineers
IF, if, intermediate frequency
IFC, International Finance
 Corporation
ill., illus., illustrated; illustration
imp., import; important; imperative
in, inch
inc., incl., inclosure; including;
 inclusive
Inc., Incorporated
incog. (incognito), in secret,
 unknown
ind., independent; indicative; index;
 industry
indef., indefinite
inf., information; infinitive; interior;
 infantry
in-lb, inch-pound
ins., inches; inspector; insurance
INS, International News Service
insp., inspected; inspector
inst., institute; institution; instant
int., interest; interior; internal
inv., inventor; invoice

invt., inventory
I/O, input/output
IQ, intelligence quotient
IRC, International Red Cross
IRE, Institute of Radio Engineers
IRS, Internal Revenue Service
ital., italics
ITO, International Trade
 Organization

j, joule
J., Journal; Judge; Justice
J/A, joint account
JAMA, Journal of the American
 Medical Association
jato, jet-assisted takeoff
J.D., Doctor of Laws
jour., journal; journalism
J.P., Justice of the Peace
Jr., Junior
jt., jnt., joint
J/T, joint tenants
junc., junction

k, kt, carat; kilogram; knot
K, Kelvin; potassium
kc, kilocycle
Kev, kilo electron volts
kg, keg; kilogram
kl, kiloliter
km, kilometer
K of C, Knights of Columbus
kt, carat; kiloton; knot
kv, kilovolt
kv-a, kilovolt-ampere
kw, kilowatt
kw-hr, kilowatt-hour

l, L, latitude; left; line; liter; length
L, pound sterling; elevated railroad;

longitude
lab., laboratory
lat., latitude
Lat., Latin
lb, pound
LC, L/C, letter of credit; Library of Congress
lc, lowercase
l.c.d., least common denominator
LCL, lcl, less-than-carload lot
LCM, least common multiple
ld, land; limited
LD, lethal dose
lect., lecture; lecturer
Legis., Legislature
lf, lightface
LF, low frequency
lib., book; library; librarian
liq., liquid; liquor
liter., literary; literature
lit., liter; literal; literature
Litt.D., Doctor of Letters
LL.B., Bachelor of Laws
LL.D., Bachelor of Laws
loc. cit. (loco citato), in the place cited
log, logarithm
long., longitude
loran, long-range navigation
LOX, liquid oxygen
LPG, liquefied petroleum gas
L.S. (locus sigilli), place of the seal
l.s.t., local standard time
l.t., local time
Ltd., Limited
lv., leaf; livre
lwl, load waterline
lwm, low watermark
LWOP, leave without pay
LWP, leave with pay

m, married; masculine; meter; male; mile; minute; moon; mother
M, thousand
M., monsieur; noon; member
ma, milliampere
MA, Maritime Administration; mental age
M.A., Master of Arts
mag., magazine; magnitude
mas., masc., m., masculine
M.A.T., Masters in the Art of Teaching
math., mathematics; -ical
max., maximum
mb, millibar
M.B.A., Master of Business Administration
Mbm, Mfbm, thousand feet board measure
mc, megacycle
MC, Medical Corps; Master of Ceremonies
Mcf, thousand cubic feet
M.D., doctor of medicine
mdse., merchandise
mech., mechanic; -ical; mechanism
med., median; medical; medicine; medieval; medium
M.Ed., Master of Education
mem., member
memo, memorandum
meq, milliequivalent
Messrs., MM., Messieurs
Mev, million electron volts
mf, millifarad; *mezzo forte*; moderately loud
MF, machine finish; medium frequency; mill finish; motor freight
M.F.A., Master of Fine Arts

LIST OF ABBREVIATIONS

mfd, manufactured; microfared
mfg., manufacturing
mfr., manufacture; manufacturer
mg, margin; milligram
mG, milligauss
MG, machine glazed; mill glazed
Mgr., Manager
mh, millihenry
mi, mile; minute; mill; mills
mid., middle
min., minimum; minute; minor
misc., miscellaneous
ml, milliliter; mail
MLD, minimum lethal dose
Mlle., Mademoiselle; Miss
mm, millimeter
M.M., Maelzel's Metronome;
  Master of Music
Mm, mym, myriameter
Mme., Mmes., Madame;
  Mesdames
mmf, magnetomotive force
mmfd, micromicrofarad
mo., month
m.o., mail order; money order
mod., moderate; modern
mol-wt, molecular weight
mp, melting point
M.P., Member of Parliament;
  Military Police
mph, miles per hour
Mr., Mister
Mrs., Mistress; Madam
ms, megasecond
M.S., Master of Science; multiple
  sclerosis
ms., mss., manuscript; manuscripts
msec, millisecond
msgr., messenger; monsignor
msl, mean sea level

M.S.N., Master of Science in
  Nursing
M.S.W., Master of Social Work
m.s.t., mountain standard time
m.t., mountain time
mtg., mtge., mortgage
mun., municipal
mus., museum; music; musical
Mus.D., Doctor of Music
m.v., market value; mean variation
M/V, motor vessel
mya, myriare
myg, myriagram
myl, myrialiter
mym, Mm, myriameter
myth., mythology

n, neutron
n., born; neuter; noun; number
N, north
n/30, net in 30 days
N.A., North America; nursing
  auxiliary
NAA, National Aeronautic
  Association
NAACP, National Association for
  the Advancement of Colored
  People
NASA, National Aeronautics and
  Space Administration
nat., national; natural; native
natl., nat'l, national
NATO, North Atlantic Treaty
  Organization
naut., nautical
nav., naval; navigation
N.B. (nota bene), note carefully
NBC, National Broadcasting
  Company
NBS, National Bureau of Standards

n.d., no date

NDAC, National Defense Advisory Commission

NE, northeast

NEA, National Education Association

neg., negative

n.f., no funds

N.F., National Formulary

NG, ng, no good; National Guard

NL, nightletter

NLRB, National Labor Relations Board

NLT, night letter cable

NM, night message

No., Nos., number; numbers

NOMA, National Office Management Association

n.o.s., not otherwise specified

non seq. (non sequitur), does not follow; not in order

NOVS, National Office of Vital Statistics

N.P., notary public; no protest; new paragraph

nr., near

NSA, National Shipping Authority

NSC, National Security Council

NSF, not sufficient funds; National Science Foundation

N.T., New Testament

nt. wt., net weight

NW, northwest; northwestern

NYP, not yet published

O, oxygen; order

OASI, old-age and survivors insurance

ob., obit., died

obj., object; objection; objective

obl., oblique; oblong

obs., obsolete; observatory

OCD, Office of Civil Defense

OD, outside diameter; outside dimensions

OEM, original equipment manufacturer

OK, OK'd, correct; approved

OP, O/P, op, out of print

op. cit. (opere citato), in the work cited

opp., opposite; opposed; opponent

O.R., o.r., owner's risk

org., organized; organic

orig., original

OS, O/S, o/s, out of stock

OSD, Office of the Secretary of Defense

O.T., Old Testament; occupational therapy

oz, ounce

p., page; **pp.,** pages; particle; part

p.a., (per annum), by the year

PA, public address system; passenger agent

Pac., Pacif., Pacific

par., paragraph; parallel; parenthesis

Pat. Off., Patent Office

pat. pend., patent pending

payt., pmt., pymt., payment

pc., piece; price; percent; postcard

P.C., Peace Corps; petty cash

PCM, punched card machines; pulse code modulation

pct, percent

pd., paid; pound

P.D. (per diem), by the day; Police Department

LIST OF ABBREVIATIONS

P.E., p.e., printer's error
pf., pfd., preferred; picofard
pF, water energy (p, logarithm; F, frequency)
pH, hydrogen-ion concentration
PHA, Public Housing Administration
Phar.D., Doctor of Pharmacy
Ph.B., B.Ph., Bachelor of Philosophy
Ph.D., D.Ph., Doctor of Philosophy
Ph.G., Graduate in Pharmacy
PHS, Public Health Service
Phys., physical; physician; physics; physiology
pk., pack; park; peck
pkg., package
pl., plate; plural
Pl., Place (street)
PL, P/L, P&L, profit and loss
plf., plff., plaintiff
P.M., p.m. (post meridiem), afternoon
P.M., paymaster; postmaster; postmortem; Prime Minister
pmkd., postmarked
P/N, p.n., promissory note; please note
P.O., p.o., postal order; post office; purchase order
P.O.B., post office box
poc, port of call
POD, pay on delivery; Post Office Department
pol., polit., politics; political
POR, pay on return
pos., possession; position; positive
poss., possession; possessive

pot., potential
pp., pages
P.P., p.p., parcel post
PP, pellagra preventive (factor)
ppd., prepaid
ppm, parts per million
P.P.S., post postscript
pr., pair; price; preferred
pref., preface; prefix
prep., preposition; preparation
Pres., President
prim., primary
prin., princ., principal; principle
prob., problem
Proc., Proceedings
prod., produce; produced; product
Prof., Professor
pron., pronoun; pronounced; pronunciation
prop., property; proposition; proprietary; proprietor; proper
pro tem (pro tempore), for the time being
prox. (proximo), in the next month
prs., pairs
P.S., postscript
psf, pounds per square foot
psi, pounds per square inch
psia, pounds per square inch absolute
psych. or psychol., psychological; psychologist; psychology
P.s.t., Pacific standard time
P.t., Pacific time
pt., part; pint; point; port
PTA, Parent-Teacher Association
ptg., printing
pto, please turn over
pub., public; -ations; publish; -er
pvt., private

pwt, pennyweight

q., qq., question; questions; query
q, qt, quart
qr, quarter; quire
qt, quart; quantity
qtr, quart., quarter; quarterly
ques., question
quot., quotation
q.v. (quo vide), which see
qy, query

r, radium dosage; right; radius; residence
R., Réaumur; River
racon, radar beacon
radar, radio detection and ranging
R.C., Red Cross; Reserve Corps
R&D, RD, research and development
rato, rocket-assisted takeoff
Rd., Road
re, with regard to
REA, Rural Electrification Administration
rec., receipt; receiver; recommended; record; recorder
recd., received
rec. sec., recording secretary
ref., referee; reference; referred; refinery; refund
refd., referred; reformed
reg., registered; regular; regulation
rep, repair; report; representative; reporter
Rep., Republication; Representative; Republic
req., requisition
retd., returned
rev., revelation; reverend; revised; reverse; revolution
Rev. Stat., Revised Statutes
RF, rf., radio frequency
RFD, rural free delivery
Rh, Rhesus (blood factor)
Riv., River
rm, ream; room
rms, root mean square
R.N., Registered Nurse
ROP, run of paper
rpm, revolutions per minute
rps, revolutions per second
RR, Railroad
RRB, Railroad Retirement Board
RSVP, please answer
Rt. Rev., Right Reverend
R.V., Revised Version
Rwy., Railway

s, second; shilling; son; section; soprano
S, south
S.A., South America
SAE, Society of Automotive Engineers
SAT, Scholastic Aptitude Test
S.B., Bachelor of Science
SBA, Small Business Administration
s and sc, sized and supercalendered
sc, sized and calendered
sc, scale; science
sc, sm. caps, small capital letters
SC, sc (scilicet), namely (see SS)
Sc.D., Doctor of Science
Sci, science; scientific
s.d. (sine die), without date
SE, southeast
SEATO, Southeast Asia Treaty Organization

144

LIST OF ABBREVIATIONS

sec, secant; second
sec., sect., section
sec., secy., secretary
SEC, Securities and Exchange
  Commission
sec-ft, second-foot
sech, hyperbolic secant
2d, 3d; 2nd, 3rd, second, third
Sen., Senate; Senator
sep., separate; sepal
seq., the following; sequel
ser., series
Sf, Svedberg flotation
s.g., sp. gr., specific gravity
sgd., signed
sh., share
SHF, superhigh frequency
shoran, short range (radio)
shp., shaft horsepower
shpt., shpmt., shipment
shtg., shortage
sic, thus; exactly as shown
sig., mark; label; signature
sin, sine
sing., singular
sinh, hyperbolic sine
sld., sealed; sold
S.M., Master of Science
so., south; southern
SO, S/O, so, seller's option
soc., society
sociol., sociology; sociologist
sofar, sound fixing and ranging
sol., solution; solicitor
sonar, sound, navigation and
  ranging
SOP, standard operating procedure
S O S, wireless distress signal
s.p. (sine prole), without issue
Sp., Spaniard; Spanish

SPCA, Society for the Prevention
  of Cruelty to Animals
spec., special; specific
Sq., Square (street)
sq-in, or in², square inch
Sr., Senior; Señor
SRO, standing room only
SS, steamship; secret service
SS, ss (scilicet), namely (see SC)
SSA, Social Security Administration
SSF, standard Saybolt furol
SSI, Supplemental Security Income
SSU, standard Saybolt universal
St., Street
St., Ste., SS., Saint; Sainte (f.);
  Saints
sta., station; stationary; stator
stacc., staccato; detached
stat., statuary; statue; statute
std., standard; steward
std-cf, standard cubic foot (feet)
stk., stock
sub., substitute; suburb; subway
subch., subchapter
subj., subject
subpar., subparagraph
subsec., subsection
SUNFED, Special United Nations
  Fund for Economic Development
sup., superior; supply
supp., suppl., supplement
supt., superintendent; support
supv., supervise
supvr., supervisor
surg., surgeon; -ery; -ical
SUS, Saybolt universal second
S.V.P., if you please
SW, southwest
sym., symbol
syn., synonym

145

syst., system

t., teaspoon; temperature
t., tp., twp., township
T, ton (s)
tan, tangent
tanh, hyperbolic tangent
TB, tuberculosis
TB, T/B, tb, trial balance
tbs. or tbsp, tablespoonful
tech., technical; technician; technology
tel, telegram; -graph; telephone
temp., temporary; temperature
ten., tenor
Ter., Terrace (street)
term., terminal; termination
tit.,title
tm, true mean
TM, transverse mercator
T/M, telemetry
TNT, trinitrotoluol
tr., transfer; translate; transpose; treasurer; trustee; transitive
trans., transaction(s); transfer
transp., transportation
treas., treasurer; treasury
TV, television
TVA, Tennessee Valley Authority
twp., t., tp., township
TWS, timed wire service (telegraph)
ty. or ter., territory

u., uncle; unit
u&lc, upper and lowercase
uc, uppercase
UGT, urgent
UHF, ultrahigh frequency
ult. (ultimo), in the last month; ultimately
U.N., United Nations
UNESCO, United Nations Educational, Scientific, and Cultural Organization
UNICEF, United Nations Children's Fund
univ., universal; university
UP, United Press
URA, Urban Renewal Administration
USA, U.S. Army
U.S.A., United States of America; Union of South Africa
U.S.C. Supp., United States Code Supplement
U.S.D.A, United States Department of Agriculture
U.S.E.S., U.S. Employment Service
U.S.I.A., U.S. Information Agency
U.S.O., United Service Organization
U.S.P., United States Pharmacopoeia
U.S.P.O., United States Post Office
U.S.S., United States Senate; United States ship
U.S.S.R., Union of Soviet Socialist Republics
u.t., universal time

v, value; vapor; verse; volt; verb; vector
v., vs. (versus), against
VA, Veterans' Administration
var., variable; variation; variegated; variety; variometer; various
VAR, visual-aural range; voltampere reactive

LIST OF ABBREVIATIONS

VD, vd, vapor density; various dates; veneral disease

vet., veteran; veterinarian; veterinary

V.F.W., Veterans of Foreign Wars

VHP, very high frequency

VIP, very important person

vid. (vide), see

VISTA, Volunteers in Service to America

viz. (videlicet), namely

VLF, very low frequency

V.M.D., Doctor of Veterinary Medicine

vocab., vocabulary

vol, volume; volunteer

vv, verses; vice versa; volumes

w, watt; with; wife; width

W, west; western

WB, W/B, wb, way bill

wd., ward; word

wf, wrong font

WG, wire guage

WHO, World Health Organization

w-hr, watt-hour

whsle., wholesale

w.i., when issued

wk, week; work

wkly., weekly

wl, wavelength; water line

w/o, without

w.o.c., without compensation

wt, warrant; weight

w.w., warehouse warrent

x, unknown quantity

XD, xd, x-div., ex-div., ex-dividend

XL, extra large

Xmas, Christmas

yd, yard; yards

YMCA, Young Men's Christian Association

YPO, Young Presidents' Organization

yr, yeal; younger; your

yrs., years; yours

YWCA, Young Women's Christian Association

z., zero

Z, zo., zone

zool., zoology; -ical; -ist

Chapter 14

POST OFFICE INFORMATION

Air Mail: The post office now moves all first-class mail within distant cities in the United States by air. Do not waste money by sending letters within the United States via airmail. However, much time can be saved by sending letters and packages to foreign countries (including Canada and Mexico) by air. To overseas countries, regular mail by sea may take one to three months for delivery. By airmail, delivery will usually take place in one to three weeks. If time is important, it may pay to send even some bulky materials by airmail. Air-freight companies or export brokers can give you information about shipping materials and supplies by air using their services.

Bulk Rate: See Third-class Mail.

Bulk Mail: If your company, club, etc. makes simultaneous mailings of fifty or more items with any frequency, you can secure a bulk mail permit. Items that carry a permit or are meter stamped and presorted by postal zones may be mailed at a special reduced rate. Larger mailings receive still lower rates. Since rates change from time to time, check with your postoffice for specific rates and requirements.

Business Reply Permits: If your company is making large mailings to secure orders or to seek a reply, you

POST OFFICE INFORMATION

generally can increase response by paying the return postage. Rather than apply postage to each return envelope or card (which is costly since many envelopes will not be returned), businesses or individuals can secure business reply permits by paying an annual fee. The envelopes must carry certain insignia and facing identification marks (series of horizontal and vertical bars) printed from negatives that are available free at the post office. Upon return of envelopes or cards the regular postage is paid plus an extra fee which almost doubles the total postage. However, postage is paid only for items actually returned.

C.O.D. Mail: First-, third-, and fourth-class mail may be sent *collect on delivery*. The post office carrier collects the amount due from the receiver at the time of delivery. The sender must prepay the postage and a collection fee. However, the mailer may include the charges in the amount to be collected from the addressee.

Insurance is included in the fee, and a return receipt may be requested. The addressee (receiver) is not allowed to inspect the contents before paying for the item.

Certified Mail: First-class mailings in the U.S. of items having no insurance value but for which assured delivery is desired may be sent *certified mail*. Delivery may be restricted to the addressee (only the addressee may sign for it) by writing the words *Restricted Delivery* above the address. A return receipt showing the addressee's signature and date of delivery may also be requested. There is an extra fee for these services.

Electronic-mail System: The U.S. Post Office provides a system whereby businesses may send communications through government computers. E-COM (Electronic-Computer Originated Mail) accepts material up to two pages in length for mailing to multiple addresses. Messages are routed to an E-Com center where they are placed in local mail for the next scheduled delivery. There is an annual subscriber fee plus a per page charge. A somewhat similar service is available through Western Union where the same letter can be sent to multiple addressees with next day delivery by mail.

Express Mail: Any item from a letter to a 70-pound package may be mailed from a designated post office (ask the post office for a list) before 5:00 p.m. with delivery guaranteed by 3:00 p.m. the next day (except Sunday). Or, if addressed to someone in care of a post office, the addressee may pick up the item at any time after 10:00 a.m. Postage is determined by weight and distance and the cost is relatively high. However, the post office refunds the full amount if delivery is made later than promised. Special labels and envelopes for this service are available at your post office. Private air-express companies also offer the same service.

First-class mail: Letters, bills, checks, receipts, orders, etc. as well as post cards must be mailed first-class mail.

POST OFFICE INFORMATION

Postage on the first ounce is the price of a regular first-class stamp with slightly lower rates for additional ounces. Inter-city mail of any distance is sent by air without extra charge. The weight limit is 70 pounds with a size limitation from 2 by $4^1/_4$ inches to a maximum of 100 inches in combined length and girth (the measurement around the package).

Stamp all large envelopes and packages *first-class* so that post office employees will not mistake them as being third-class. First-class mail, such as letters, may be included in second-, third-, or fourth-class mail provided you note on the outside of the package *letter enclosed*, etc. and affix the additional first-class postage to the package. Or you may attach a stamped envelope containing a letter, etc. to the outside of the package. Any item weighing more than 12 ounces is classified as *priority mail*, described later in this section.

Fourth-class Mail (Parcel Post): Items weighing 16 ounces or more and not shipped first-, second-, or third-class mail are designated *Parcel Post*. Postage is based on weight and distance. Weight cannot exceed 70 pounds and size cannot exceed 108 inces of combined length and girth (distance around the package).

Special delivery is available for fourth-class mail. However, sending a package by priority mail (first-class mail) is oftentimes better and less costly then fourth-class, special delivery.

Special fourth-class rates are available for books, educational materials, manuscripts, catalogs, films, records, etc. Check with your post office for details.

General Delivery: For persons not permanently located in a city, mail may be sent to the destination post office in that person's name. Write *General Delivery* above the person's name and then the post office (or a specific branch) address (city, state, and zip code). The person addressed will have to call at the post office and provide identification to secure his mail.

Insured Mail: Insured mail is available for only third- and fourth class mail. In the event of loss, the post office will pay only the cost value of the item sent.

International Mail: First-class mail, air mail, and parcel post service are available to other countries. However, the rates and mailing rules vary from country to country. Check with your post office for the specific rates, etc. for the country to which you are mailing. A copy of *International Postage Rates and Fees* may also be secured from the U.S. Postal Service without charge.

POST OFFICE INFORMATION

Metered Mail: Small businesses may buy or rent manual meters. However, larger businesses usually have electically powered meter machines that automatically feed, seal, meter-stamp, and count the mail. The sealed meter box is taken to the post office to replenish the postage.

Money Order: A *postal money order* for up to $500 may be purchased or cashed at any U.S. post office.

National Zip Code Directory: A large directory listing zip codes by state, city, and street may be secured at any post office for a nominal fee.

Parcel Post: See fourth-class mail.

Post Cards: Cards ranging in size from $3^1/_2$ by 5 inches to $4^1/_4$ by 6 inches may be mailed at rates lower than first-class envelope mail. A post card carrying first-class prepaid postage may be purchased at your local post office.

Post Office Box: Boxes or bins may be rented at any post office. A box enables a business or individual to pick up mail at anytime that post office lobbies are open. Many larger businesses may rent several boxes so that their mail is automatically presorted by box number (such as for payments, new orders, sales reports, etc.).

Priority Mail (Air Parcel Post): All first-class mail weighing from 13 ounces to 70 pounds is classified as *Priority Mail*. Priority mail receives air service the same as other first-class mail.

Registered Mail: First-class mail that is registered is kept locked and separate from other mail. It is the safest way for mailing valuable documents or other papers that are uninsurable. All items that are irreplaceable or difficult to replace should be registered (such as money, stock certificates, manuscripts, signed documents, jewelry of unusual value, etc.).

At the time of mailing, the sender receives a numbered receipt and the post office maintains a record of the number. As proof of delivery a return receipt may be requested.

In addition, to first-class postage and return receipt fee, the sender must pay a registration fee based on the declared value (up to $10,000) of the item.

Second-class Mail: This mail class provides special rates for publishers who have permits to mail magazines or newspapers, for publications of certain non-profit organizations, or for individuals mailing complete publications. The wrapper must be marked *second-class* and no other communication may be included without making all the items subject to first-class postage.

POST OFFICE INFORMATION

Special Delivery: A special delivery fee may be paid for all classes of mail. For this fee, in addition to regular postage, delivery is assured immediately after arrival at the destination post office.

Third-class Mail: This class mail may be used for individual or bulk mailings of advertising material such as booklets, circulars, and catalogs, and for merchandise, seeds, bulbs, and plants that weigh less than 16 ounces apiece. Items weighing more than 16 ounces are classified as fourth-class (parcel post). Third-class mail must be left unsealed for postal inspection, or if sealed, marked *bulk mail* or *third-class mail*. it must not include written messages or directions on the outside. Check with your post office for the specific requirements for the type of item you are mailing.

Chapter 15

TIME CHANGE

Business today in many industries is done on a worldwide basis. Government and military personnel, too, often must communicate with others in many foreign countries. There is often a need, then, for knowing the time in other locations or other travel itineraries. The listings on the pages which follow will enable you to quickly determine the time in other locations.

In the listing, if all of a country is in one time zone, only the name of the country is given. Where there is more than one zone, the principal cities of the country are given with their time zone.

The *Eastern Standard Time* Zone in the United States is used as a base. If you are in that zone, you only need to add or subtract the number of hours indicated after the name of the country or city whose time you are determining.

For example, if you are in New York or New Jersey or any other Eastern Time Zone area, and wish to know the time in Rome, Italy, look up *Italy*. You will find it has only one time zone indicated as +6. Simply add 6 hours to your time. In other words, if it is 12 o'clock where you are, it is 6 p.m. in Rome.

If you are not in the Eastern Standard Time Zone, follow these steps:

1. In the list, find the name of the country or city *where you are* or near.
2. Reverse the sign given for your location; e.g. change a +3 to a −3. Then add or subtract that number from the actual time where you are.
3. Find the name of the country whose time you wish to know and add or subtract the figure you arrived at in step 2 above.

For example, if you are in San Francisco and wish to know the time in Hong Kong when your time is 2 p.m.:

1. Locate San Francisco in the list.
2. Change the −3 to +3 and then add that amount to your actual time. Your time 2 p.m. plus 3 = 5 p.m.
3. Look up Hong Kong which shows + 13. Add that amount to the time from step 2 above: 5 p.m. + 13 = 18 or, in other words, it would be 11 a.m. in Hong Kong when the time is 2 p.m. in San Francisco.

Note: If Daylight Savings Time is in effect in your time zone, *subtract* one hour from the result you found by following the steps above. In the example above, you would subtract one hour from 6 a.m. making it 5 a.m. You would then not want to call until after 5 p.m. San Francisco time to reach someone in Hong Kong after 8 a.m.

Afghanistan $+9^{1}/_{2}$

Algeria $+6$

Angola $+6$

Argentina $+1$

Australia

   Adelaide $+14^{1}/_{2}$

   Brisbane $+15$

   Canberra $+15$

   Darwin $+14^{1}/_{2}$

   Melbourne $+15$

   Perth $+13$

   Sydney $+15$

Austria $+6$

Bangladesh $+11$

Barbados $+1$

Belgium $+6$

Bolivia $+1$

Botswana $+7$

Brazil

Belo Horizonte $+2$

Brasilia $+2$

Campo Grande $+1$

Recife $+2$

Pôrto Velho $+1$

Rio de Janeiro $+2$

Sao Luis $+2$

Sao Paulo $+2$

Bulgaria $+7$

Burma $+11^{1}/_{2}$

Burundi $+7$

Cambodia $+12$

Cameroon $+6$

Canada

   Montreal 0

   Ottawa 0

   Toronto 0

   Vancouver -3

   Winnipeg -1

TIME CHANGE

Central Africa
  Republic +6
Chad +6
Chile +1
China +13
Columbia 0
Congo, Rep. of +6
Costa Rica −1
Cuba 0
Cyprus +6
Czechoslovakia +6
Dahomey +6
Denmark +6
Dominican Rep. 0
Ecuador 0
Egypt +7
El Salvador −1
Equatorial
  Guinea +6
Ethiopia +8
Finland +7
France +6
Gabon +6
Gambia +5
Germany, East +6
Germany, West +6
Ghana +5

Greece +7
Greenland +2
Guatemala −1
Guinea +5
Guyana +2
Haiti 0
Honduras −1
Hong Kong +13
Hungary +6
Iceland +4
India +10$\frac{1}{2}$
Indonesia
  Bandung +12
  Djakarta +12
  Irian Jaya +14
  Semarang +13
  Surabaya +12
Iran +8$\frac{1}{2}$
Iraq +8
Ireland +6
Italy +6
Ivory Coast +5
Jamaica 0
Japan +14
Jordan +7
Kenya +8
Korea +14

Kuwait +8
Laos +12
Lebanon +7
Lesotho +7
Liberia + 5³/₄
Libya +7
Luxembourg +6
Malagasy Rep. +8
Malawi +7
Malasia +12¹/₂
Maldive Is. +10
Mali +5
Malta +6
Mauritania +5
Mauritius +9
Mexico
  Guadalajara −1
  Mexico City −1
  Monterey −1
  Mazatlán −2
Mongolian Rep. +13
Morocco +5
Nepal +10¹/₂
Netherlands +6
Newfoundland +1¹/₂
New Zealand +17
Nicaragua −1

Niger + 6
Nigeria +6
Nova Scotia +1
Pakistan +10
Panama 0
Paraguay +1
Peru 0
Philippines +13
Poland +6
Portugal +6
Rhodesia +7
Rumania +7
Samoa, W. −6
Saudia Arabia +9
Senegal +5
Singapore + 12¹/₂
Somalia +8
South Africa +7
Spain +6
Sri Lanka +10¹/₂
Sudan +7
Sweden +6
Switzerland +6
Syria +7
Taiwan +13
Tanzania +8
Thailand +12

TIME CHANGE

Togo Rep. +5
Trinidad and
  Tobago +1
Tunisia +6
Turkey +7
Uganda +8
USSR
  Alma-Ata +11
  Baku +9
  Gorki +9
  Kharkov +8
  Kiev +8
  Kuybyshev +9
  Leningrad +8
  Minsk +8
  Moscow +8
  Novosibirsk +12
  Odessa +8
  Omsk +12
  Perm +12
  Rija +8
  Rostov +9
  Tashkent +11
  Vladivostok +15
  Volgograd +9
United Kingdom +6

United States
  Anchorage −5
  Atlanta 0
  Baltimore 0
  Boston 0
  Buffalo 0
  Chicago −1
  Cincinnati 0
  Cleveland 0
  Columbus 0
  Dallas −1
  Denver −2
  Detroit 0
  Ft. Worth −1
  Honolulu −5
  Houston −1
  Indianapolis −1
  Kansas City −1
  Memphis −1
  Minneapolis −1
  New York 0
  Los Angeles −3
  Milwaukee −1
  New Orleans −1
  Oklahoma City −1
  Phoenix −2

Pittsburgh 0
Philadelphia 0
St. Louis − 1
San Antonio − 1
San Francisco − 3
Seattle − 3
Washington 0
Upper Volta + 5
Uruguay + 2

Venezuela + 1
Vietnam + 13
Yemen + 8
Yugoslavia + 6
Zaire
   Kinshasa + 6
   Lumbumbashi + 7
Zambia + 7

Chapter 16

ROMAN NUMERALS

Roman numerals are not widely used, but used often enough so you should be able to read or interpret them. Following is a table of Arabic numerals and their equivalent Roman Numerals.

Table of Roman Numerals

Arabic Numeral	Roman Numeral	Arabic Numeral	Roman Numeral
1	I	50	L
2	II	60	LX
3	III	70	LXX
4	IV	80	LXXX
5	V	90	XC
6	VI	100	C
7	VII	200	CC
8	VIII	300	CCC
9	IX	400	CD
10	X	500	D
11	XI	600	DC
12	XII	700	DCC
13	XIII	800	DCCC
14	XIV	900	CM
15	XV	1,000	M
16	XVI	4,000	$M\overline{V}$
17	XVII	5,000	$\overline{V}$
18	XVII	10,000	$\overline{X}$
19	XIX	15,000	$\overline{XV}$
20	XX	20,000	$\overline{XX}$
30	XXX	100,000	$\overline{C}$
40	XL	1,000,000	$\overline{M}$

The following examples illustrate the use and meaning of Roman Numerals.

1. A Roman Numeral or letter preceding *a letter of greater value* subtracts from it:

$$V = 5 \qquad IV = 4$$
$$L = 50 \qquad XL = 40$$
$$C = 100 \qquad XC = 90$$

2. A letter preceding *a letter of equal or lesser value* adds to it.

$$V = 5 \qquad VI = 6$$
$$L = 50 \qquad LX = 60$$
$$C = 100 \qquad CXI = 111$$

3. You will quickly, of course, be able to remember and recognize smaller numbers.

XVI = 16
X (10) + VI (6) = 16
XLIV = 44
XL (40) + IV (4) = 44
XCI = 91
XC (90) + I (1) = 91

ROMAN NUMERALS

For larger numbers simply examine the numbers and break it down into its elements and you will readily interpret the number. You will be able to recognize the elements or parts by applying rules 1 and 2 given above or by looking at the table of Roman Numerals.

CDXCIII = 493
  CD (400) + XC (90) + III (3) = 493
DCXCIX = 699
  DC (600) + XC (90) + IX (9) = 699
MDCLXXV = 1,675
  M (1,000) + DC (600) + LXX (70)
    + V (5) = 1,675

4. A bar over a Roman Numeral multiplies it by 1,000.

$$M\overline{V} = 4,000 \qquad \overline{V} = 5,000$$
$$\overline{X}\overline{V} = 15,000 \qquad \overline{X}\overline{X} = 20,000$$

Chapter 17

PERPETUAL CALENDAR

The use of this perpetual calendar will enable you to determine the day of the week on which any date fell or will fall during the two centuries from 1901 to 2100. To locate a date and day of the week, first locate the year in which you are interested in the list below. Following the year is a letter to tell you which calendar to use on the pages which follow. In addition, if you are planning schedules, etc. for the next year or two and do not yet have copies of those calendars, simply look up the year and the calendar letter, and you will then have a calendar for the entire year in question.

1901 C	1915 F	1929 C	1943 F
1902 D	1916 N	1930 D	1944 N
1903 E	1917 B	1931 E	1945 B
1904 M	1918 C	1932 M	1946 C
1905 A	1919 D	1933 A	1947 D
1906 B	1920 L	1934 B	1948 L
1907 C	1921 G	1935 C	1949 G
1908 K	1922 A	1936 K	1950 A
1909 F	1923 B	1937 F	1951 B
1910 G	1924 J	1938 G	1952 J
1911 A	1925 E	1939 A	1953 E
1912 I	1926 F	1940 I	1954 F
1913 D	1927 G	1941 D	1955 G
1914 E	1928 H	1942 E	1956 H

PERPETUAL CALENDAR

1957 C	1993 F	2029 B	2065 E
1958 D	1994 G	2030 C	2066 F
1959 E	1995 A	2031 D	2067 G
1960 M	1996 I	2032 L	2068 H
1961 A	1997 D	2033 G	2069 C
1962 B	1998 E	2034 A	2070 D
1963 C	1999 F	2035 B	2071 E
1964 K	2000 N	2036 J	2072 M
1965 F	2001 B	2037 E	2073 A
1966 G	2002 C	2038 F	2074 B
1967 A	2003 D	2039 G	2075 C
1968 I	2004 L	2040 H	2076 K
1969 D	2005 G	2041 C	2077 F
1970 E	2006 A	2042 D	2078 G
1971 F	2007 B	2043 E	2079 A
1972 N	2008 J	2044 M	2080 I
1973 B	2009 E	2045 A	2081 D
1974 C	2010 F	2046 B	2082 E
1975 D	2011 G	2047 C	2083 F
1976 L	2012 H	2048 K	2084 N
1977 G	2013 C	2049 F	2085 B
1978 A	2014 D	2050 G	2086 C
1979 B	2015 E	2051 A	2087 D
1980 J	2016 M	2052 I	2088 L
1981 E	2017 A	2053 D	2089 G
1982 F	2018 B	2054 E	2090 A
1983 G	2019 C	2055 F	2091 B
1984 H	2020 K	2056 N	2092 J
1985 C	2021 F	2057 B	2093 E
1986 D	2022 G	2058 C	2094 F
1987 E	2023 A	2059 D	2095 G
1988 M	2024 I	2060 L	2096 H
1989 A	2025 D	2061 G	2097 C
1990 B	2026 E	2062 A	2098 D
1991 C	2027 F	2063 B	2099 E
1992 K	2028 N	2064 J	2100 F

A

JANUARY

S	M	T	W	T	F	S
1	2	3	4	5	6	7
8	9	10	11	12	13	14
15	16	17	18	19	20	21
22	23	24	25	26	27	28
29	30	31				

MAY

S	M	T	W	T	F	S
	1	2	3	4	5	6
7	8	9	10	11	12	13
14	15	16	17	18	19	20
21	22	23	24	25	26	27
28	29	30	31			

SEPTEMBER

S	M	T	W	T	F	S
					1	2
3	4	5	6	7	8	9
10	11	12	13	14	15	16
17	18	19	20	21	22	23
24	25	26	27	28	29	30

FEBRUARY

S	M	T	W	T	F	S
			1	2	3	4
5	6	7	8	9	10	11
12	13	14	15	16	17	18
19	20	21	22	23	24	25
26	27	28				

JUNE

S	M	T	W	T	F	S
				1	2	3
4	5	6	7	8	9	10
11	12	13	14	15	16	17
18	19	20	21	22	23	24
25	26	27	28	29	30	

OCTOBER

S	M	T	W	T	F	S
1	2	3	4	5	6	7
8	9	10	11	12	13	14
15	16	17	18	19	20	21
22	23	24	25	26	27	28
29	30	31				

MARCH

S	M	T	W	T	F	S
			1	2	3	4
5	6	7	8	9	10	11
12	13	14	15	16	17	18
19	20	21	22	23	24	25
26	27	28	29	30	31	

JULY

S	M	T	W	T	F	S
						1
2	3	4	5	6	7	8
9	10	11	12	13	14	15
16	17	18	19	20	21	22
23	24	25	26	27	28	29
30	31					

NOVEMBER

S	M	T	W	T	F	S
			1	2	3	4
5	6	7	8	9	10	11
12	13	14	15	16	17	18
19	20	21	22	23	24	25
26	27	28	29	30		

APRIL

S	M	T	W	T	F	S
						1
2	3	4	5	6	7	8
9	10	11	12	13	14	15
16	17	18	19	20	21	22
23	24	25	26	27	28	29
30						

AUGUST

S	M	T	W	T	F	S
		1	2	3	4	5
6	7	8	9	10	11	12
13	14	15	16	17	18	19
20	21	22	23	24	25	26
27	28	29	30	31		

DECEMBER

S	M	T	W	T	F	S
					1	2
3	4	5	6	7	8	9
10	11	12	13	14	15	16
17	18	19	20	21	22	23
24	25	26	27	28	29	30
31						

B

JANUARY

S	M	T	W	T	F	S
	1	2	3	4	5	6
7	8	9	10	11	12	13
14	15	16	17	18	19	20
21	22	23	24	25	26	27
28	29	30	31			

MAY

S	M	T	W	T	F	S
		1	2	3	4	5
6	7	8	9	10	11	12
13	14	15	16	17	18	19
20	21	22	23	24	25	26
27	28	29	30	31		

SEPTEMBER

S	M	T	W	T	F	S
						1
2	3	4	5	6	7	8
9	10	11	12	13	14	15
16	17	18	19	20	21	22
23	24	25	26	27	28	29
30						

FEBRUARY

S	M	T	W	T	F	S
				1	2	3
4	5	6	7	8	9	10
11	12	13	14	15	16	17
18	19	20	21	22	23	24
25	26	27	28			

JUNE

S	M	T	W	T	F	S
					1	2
3	4	5	6	7	8	9
10	11	12	13	14	15	16
17	18	19	20	21	22	23
24	25	26	27	28	29	30

OCTOBER

S	M	T	W	T	F	S
	1	2	3	4	5	6
7	8	9	10	11	12	13
14	15	16	17	18	19	20
21	22	23	24	25	26	27
28	29	30	31			

MARCH

S	M	T	W	T	F	S
				1	2	3
4	5	6	7	8	9	10
11	12	13	14	15	16	17
18	19	20	21	22	23	24
25	26	27	28	29	30	31

JULY

S	M	T	W	T	F	S
1	2	3	4	5	6	7
8	9	10	11	12	13	14
15	16	17	18	19	20	21
22	23	24	25	26	27	28
29	30	31				

NOVEMBER

S	M	T	W	T	F	S
				1	2	3
4	5	6	7	8	9	10
11	12	13	14	15	16	17
18	19	20	21	22	23	24
25	26	27	28	29	30	

APRIL

S	M	T	W	T	F	S
1	2	3	4	5	6	7
8	9	10	11	12	13	14
15	16	17	18	19	20	21
22	23	24	25	26	27	28
29	30					

AUGUST

S	M	T	W	T	F	S
			1	2	3	4
5	6	7	8	9	10	11
12	13	14	15	16	17	18
19	20	21	22	23	24	25
26	27	28	29	30	31	

DECEMBER

S	M	T	W	T	F	S
						1
2	3	4	5	6	7	8
9	10	11	12	13	14	15
16	17	18	19	20	21	22
23	24	25	26	27	28	29
30	31					

PERPETUAL CALENDAR

C

JANUARY

S	M	T	W	T	F	S
		1	2	3	4	5
6	7	8	9	10	11	12
13	14	15	16	17	18	19
20	21	22	23	24	25	26
27	28	29	30	31		

FEBRUARY

S	M	T	W	T	F	S
					1	2
3	4	5	6	7	8	9
10	11	12	13	14	15	16
17	18	19	20	21	22	23
24	25	26	27	28		

MARCH

S	M	T	W	T	F	S
					1	2
3	4	5	6	7	8	9
10	11	12	13	14	15	16
17	18	19	20	21	22	23
24	25	26	27	28	29	30
31						

APRIL

S	M	T	W	T	F	S
	1	2	3	4	5	6
7	8	9	10	11	12	13
14	15	16	17	18	19	20
21	22	23	24	25	26	27
28	29	30				

MAY

S	M	T	W	T	F	S
			1	2	3	4
5	6	7	8	9	10	11
12	13	14	15	16	17	18
19	20	21	22	23	24	25
26	27	28	29	30	31	

JUNE

S	M	T	W	T	F	S
						1
2	3	4	5	6	7	8
9	10	11	12	13	14	15
16	17	18	19	20	21	22
23	24	25	26	27	28	29
30						

JULY

S	M	T	W	T	F	S
	1	2	3	4	5	6
7	8	9	10	11	12	13
14	15	16	17	18	19	20
21	22	23	24	25	26	27
28	29	30	31			

AUGUST

S	M	T	W	T	F	S
				1	2	3
4	5	6	7	8	9	10
11	12	13	14	15	16	17
18	19	20	21	22	23	24
25	26	27	28	29	30	31

SEPTEMBER

S	M	T	W	T	F	S
1	2	3	4	5	6	7
8	9	10	11	12	13	14
15	16	17	18	19	20	21
22	23	24	25	26	27	28
29	30					

OCTOBER

S	M	T	W	T	F	S
		1	2	3	4	5
6	7	8	9	10	11	12
13	14	15	16	17	18	19
20	21	22	23	24	25	26
27	28	29	30	31		

NOVEMBER

S	M	T	W	T	F	S
					1	2
3	4	5	6	7	8	9
10	11	12	13	14	15	16
17	18	19	20	21	22	23
24	25	26	27	28	29	30

DECEMBER

S	M	T	W	T	F	S
1	2	3	4	5	6	7
8	9	10	11	12	13	14
15	16	17	18	19	20	21
22	23	24	25	26	27	28
29	30	31				

D

JANUARY

S	M	T	W	T	F	S
			1	2	3	4
5	6	7	8	9	10	11
12	13	14	15	16	17	18
19	20	21	22	23	24	25
26	27	28	29	30	31	

FEBRUARY

S	M	T	W	T	F	S
						1
2	3	4	5	6	7	8
9	10	11	12	13	14	15
16	17	18	19	20	21	22
23	24	25	26	27	28	

MARCH

S	M	T	W	T	F	S
						1
2	3	4	5	6	7	8
9	10	11	12	13	14	15
16	17	18	19	20	21	22
23	24	25	26	27	28	29
30	31					

APRIL

S	M	T	W	T	F	S
		1	2	3	4	5
6	7	8	9	10	11	12
13	14	15	16	17	18	19
20	21	22	23	24	25	26
27	28	29	30			

MAY

S	M	T	W	T	F	S
				1	2	3
4	5	6	7	8	9	10
11	12	13	14	15	16	17
18	19	20	21	22	23	24
25	26	27	28	29	30	31

JUNE

S	M	T	W	T	F	S
1	2	3	4	5	6	7
8	9	10	11	12	13	14
15	16	17	18	19	20	21
22	23	24	25	26	27	28
29	30					

JULY

S	M	T	W	T	F	S
		1	2	3	4	5
6	7	8	9	10	11	12
13	14	15	16	17	18	19
20	21	22	23	24	25	26
27	28	29	30	31		

AUGUST

S	M	T	W	T	F	S
					1	2
3	4	5	6	7	8	9
10	11	12	13	14	15	16
17	18	19	20	21	22	23
24	25	26	27	28	29	30
31						

SEPTEMBER

S	M	T	W	T	F	S
	1	2	3	4	5	6
7	8	9	10	11	12	13
14	15	16	17	18	19	20
21	22	23	24	25	26	27
28	29	30				

OCTOBER

S	M	T	W	T	F	S
			1	2	3	4
5	6	7	8	9	10	11
12	13	14	15	16	17	18
19	20	21	22	23	24	25
26	27	28	29	30	31	

NOVEMBER

S	M	T	W	T	F	S
						1
2	3	4	5	6	7	8
9	10	11	12	13	14	15
16	17	18	19	20	21	22
23	24	25	26	27	28	29
30						

DECEMBER

S	M	T	W	T	F	S
	1	2	3	4	5	6
7	8	9	10	11	12	13
14	15	16	17	18	19	20
21	22	23	24	25	26	27
28	29	30	31			

E

JANUARY

S	M	T	W	T	F	S
				1	2	3
4	5	6	7	8	9	10
11	12	13	14	15	16	17
18	19	20	21	22	23	24
25	26	27	28	29	30	31

FEBRUARY

S	M	T	W	T	F	S
1	2	3	4	5	6	7
8	9	10	11	12	13	14
15	16	17	18	19	20	21
22	23	24	25	26	27	28

MARCH

S	M	T	W	T	F	S
1	2	3	4	5	6	7
8	9	10	11	12	13	14
15	16	17	18	19	20	21
22	23	24	25	26	27	28
29	30	31				

APRIL

S	M	T	W	T	F	S
			1	2	3	4
5	6	7	8	9	10	11
12	13	14	15	16	17	18
19	20	21	22	23	24	25
26	27	28	29	30		

MAY

S	M	T	W	T	F	S
					1	2
3	4	5	6	7	8	9
10	11	12	13	14	15	16
17	18	19	20	21	22	23
24	25	26	27	28	29	30
31						

JUNE

S	M	T	W	T	F	S
	1	2	3	4	5	6
7	8	9	10	11	12	13
14	15	16	17	18	19	20
21	22	23	24	25	26	27
28	29	30				

JULY

S	M	T	W	T	F	S
			1	2	3	4
5	6	7	8	9	10	11
12	13	14	15	16	17	18
19	20	21	22	23	24	25
26	27	28	29	30	31	

AUGUST

S	M	T	W	T	F	S
						1
2	3	4	5	6	7	8
9	10	11	12	13	14	15
16	17	18	19	20	21	22
23	24	25	26	27	28	29
30	31					

SEPTEMBER

S	M	T	W	T	F	S
		1	2	3	4	5
6	7	8	9	10	11	12
13	14	15	16	17	18	19
20	21	22	23	24	25	26
27	28	29	30			

OCTOBER

S	M	T	W	T	F	S
				1	2	3
4	5	6	7	8	9	10
11	12	13	14	15	16	17
18	19	20	21	22	23	24
25	26	27	28	29	30	31

NOVEMBER

S	M	T	W	T	F	S
1	2	3	4	5	6	7
8	9	10	11	12	13	14
15	16	17	18	19	20	21
22	23	24	25	26	27	28
29	30					

DECEMBER

S	M	T	W	T	F	S
		1	2	3	4	5
6	7	8	9	10	11	12
13	14	15	16	17	18	19
20	21	22	23	24	25	26
27	28	29	30	31		

F

JANUARY

S	M	T	W	T	F	S
					1	2
3	4	5	6	7	8	9
10	11	12	13	14	15	16
17	18	19	20	21	22	23
24	25	26	27	28	29	30
31						

FEBRUARY

S	M	T	W	T	F	S
	1	2	3	4	5	6
7	8	9	10	11	12	13
14	15	16	17	18	19	20
21	22	23	24	25	26	27
28						

MARCH

S	M	T	W	T	F	S
	1	2	3	4	5	6
7	8	9	10	11	12	13
14	15	16	17	18	19	20
21	22	23	24	25	26	27
28	29	30	31			

APRIL

S	M	T	W	T	F	S
				1	2	3
4	5	6	7	8	9	10
11	12	13	14	15	16	17
18	19	20	21	22	23	24
25	26	27	28	29	30	

MAY

S	M	T	W	T	F	S
						1
2	3	4	5	6	7	8
9	10	11	12	13	14	15
16	17	18	19	20	21	22
23	24	25	26	27	28	29
30	31					

JUNE

S	M	T	W	T	F	S
		1	2	3	4	5
6	7	8	9	10	11	12
13	14	15	16	17	18	19
20	21	22	23	24	25	26
27	28	29	30			

JULY

S	M	T	W	T	F	S
				1	2	3
4	5	6	7	8	9	10
11	12	13	14	15	16	17
18	19	20	21	22	23	24
25	26	27	28	29	30	31

AUGUST

S	M	T	W	T	F	S
1	2	3	4	5	6	7
8	9	10	11	12	13	14
15	16	17	18	19	20	21
22	23	24	25	26	27	28
29	30	31				

SEPTEMBER

S	M	T	W	T	F	S
			1	2	3	4
5	6	7	8	9	10	11
12	13	14	15	16	17	18
19	20	21	22	23	24	25
26	27	28	29	30		

OCTOBER

S	M	T	W	T	F	S
					1	2
3	4	5	6	7	8	9
10	11	12	13	14	15	16
17	18	19	20	21	22	23
24	25	26	27	28	29	30
31						

NOVEMBER

S	M	T	W	T	F	S
	1	2	3	4	5	6
7	8	9	10	11	12	13
14	15	16	17	18	19	20
21	22	23	24	25	26	27
28	29	30				

DECEMBER

S	M	T	W	T	F	S
			1	2	3	4
5	6	7	8	9	10	11
12	13	14	15	16	17	18
19	20	21	22	23	24	25
26	27	28	29	30	31	

PERPETUAL CALENDAR

G

JANUARY
S	M	T	W	T	F	S
						1
2	3	4	5	6	7	8
9	10	11	12	13	14	15
16	17	18	19	20	21	22
23	24	25	26	27	28	29
30	31					

MAY
S	M	T	W	T	F	S
1	2	3	4	5	6	7
8	9	10	11	12	13	14
15	16	17	18	19	20	21
22	23	24	25	26	27	28
29	30	31				

SEPTEMBER
S	M	T	W	T	F	S
					1	2
3	4	5	6	7	8	9
10	11	12	13	14	15	16
17	18	19	20	21	22	23
24	25	26	27	28	29	30

FEBRUARY
S	M	T	W	T	F	S
			1	2	3	4
5	6	7	8	9	10	11
12	13	14	15	16	17	18
19	20	21	22	23	24	25
26	27	28				

JUNE
S	M	T	W	T	F	S
				1	2	3
4	5	6	7	8	9	10
11	12	13	14	15	16	17
18	19	20	21	22	23	24
25	26	27	28	29	30	

OCTOBER
S	M	T	W	T	F	S
1	2	3	4	5	6	7
8	9	10	11	12	13	14
15	16	17	18	19	20	21
22	23	24	25	26	27	28
29	30	31				

MARCH
S	M	T	W	T	F	S
			1	2	3	4
5	6	7	8	9	10	11
12	13	14	15	16	17	18
19	20	21	22	23	24	25
26	27	28	29	30	31	

JULY
S	M	T	W	T	F	S
					1	2
3	4	5	6	7	8	9
10	11	12	13	14	15	16
17	18	19	20	21	22	23
24	25	26	27	28	29	30
31						

NOVEMBER
S	M	T	W	T	F	S
			1	2	3	4
5	6	7	8	9	10	11
12	13	14	15	16	17	18
19	20	21	22	23	24	25
26	27	28	29	30		

APRIL
S	M	T	W	T	F	S
						1
2	3	4	5	6	7	8
9	10	11	12	13	14	15
16	17	18	19	20	21	22
23	24	25	26	27	28	29
30						

AUGUST
S	M	T	W	T	F	S
	1	2	3	4	5	6
7	8	9	10	11	12	13
14	15	16	17	18	19	20
21	22	23	24	25	26	27
28	29	30	31			

DECEMBER
S	M	T	W	T	F	S
					1	2
3	4	5	6	7	8	9
10	11	12	13	14	15	16
17	18	19	20	21	22	23
24	25	26	27	28	29	30
31						

H

JANUARY
S	M	T	W	T	F	S
1	2	3	4	5	6	7
8	9	10	11	12	13	14
15	16	17	18	19	20	21
22	23	24	25	26	27	28
29	30	31				

MAY
S	M	T	W	T	F	S
		1	2	3	4	5
6	7	8	9	10	11	12
13	14	15	16	17	18	19
20	21	22	23	24	25	26
27	28	29	30	31		

SEPTEMBER
S	M	T	W	T	F	S
						1
2	3	4	5	6	7	8
9	10	11	12	13	14	15
16	17	18	19	20	21	22
23	24	25	26	27	28	29
30						

FEBRUARY
S	M	T	W	T	F	S
			1	2	3	4
5	6	7	8	9	10	11
12	13	14	15	16	17	18
19	20	21	22	23	24	25
26	27	28				

JUNE
S	M	T	W	T	F	S
					1	2
3	4	5	6	7	8	9
10	11	12	13	14	15	16
17	18	19	20	21	22	23
24	25	26	27	28	29	30

OCTOBER
S	M	T	W	T	F	S
1	2	3	4	5	6	
7	8	9	10	11	12	13
14	15	16	17	18	19	20
21	22	23	24	25	26	27
28	29	30	31			

MARCH
S	M	T	W	T	F	S
				1	2	3
4	5	6	7	8	9	10
11	12	13	14	15	16	17
18	19	20	21	22	23	24
25	26	27	28	29	30	31

JULY
S	M	T	W	T	F	S
1	2	3	4	5	6	7
8	9	10	11	12	13	14
15	16	17	18	19	20	21
22	23	24	25	26	27	28
29	30	31				

NOVEMBER
S	M	T	W	T	F	S
				1	2	3
4	5	6	7	8	9	10
11	12	13	14	15	16	17
18	19	20	21	22	23	24
25	26	27	28	29	30	

APRIL
S	M	T	W	T	F	S
1	2	3	4	5	6	7
8	9	10	11	12	13	14
15	16	17	18	19	20	21
22	23	24	25	26	27	28
29	30					

AUGUST
S	M	T	W	T	F	S
			1	2	3	4
5	6	7	8	9	10	11
12	13	14	15	16	17	18
19	20	21	22	23	24	25
26	27	28	29	30	31	

DECEMBER
S	M	T	W	T	F	S
						1
2	3	4	5	6	7	8
9	10	11	12	13	14	15
16	17	18	19	20	21	22
23	24	25	26	27	28	29
30	31					

I

JANUARY

S	M	T	W	T	F	S
	1	2	3	4	5	6
7	8	9	10	11	12	13
14	15	16	17	18	19	20
21	22	23	24	25	26	27
28	29	30	31			

MAY

S	M	T	W	T	F	S
		1	2	3	4	
5	6	7	8	9	10	11
12	13	14	15	16	17	18
19	20	21	22	23	24	25
26	27	28	29	30	31	

SEPTEMBER

S	M	T	W	T	F	S
1	2	3	4	5	6	7
8	9	10	11	12	13	14
15	16	17	18	19	20	21
22	23	24	25	26	27	28
29	30					

FEBRUARY

S	M	T	W	T	F	S
				1	2	3
4	5	6	7	8	9	10
11	12	13	14	15	16	17
18	19	20	21	22	23	24
25	26	27	28			

JUNE

S	M	T	W	T	F	S
						1
2	3	4	5	6	7	8
9	10	11	12	13	14	15
16	17	18	19	20	21	22
23	24	25	26	27	28	29
30						

OCTOBER

S	M	T	W	T	F	S
		1	2	3	4	5
6	7	8	9	10	11	12
13	14	15	16	17	18	19
20	21	22	23	24	25	26
27	28	29	30	31		

MARCH

S	M	T	W	T	F	S
					1	2
3	4	5	6	7	8	9
10	11	12	13	14	15	16
17	18	19	20	21	22	23
24	25	26	27	28	29	30
31						

JULY

S	M	T	W	T	F	S
	1	2	3	4	5	6
7	8	9	10	11	12	13
14	15	16	17	18	19	20
21	22	23	24	25	26	27
28	29	30	31			

NOVEMBER

S	M	T	W	T	F	S
					1	2
3	4	5	6	7	8	9
10	11	12	13	14	15	16
17	18	19	20	21	22	23
24	25	26	27	28	29	30

APRIL

S	M	T	W	T	F	S
	1	2	3	4	5	6
7	8	9	10	11	12	13
14	15	16	17	18	19	20
21	22	23	24	25	26	27
28	29	30				

AUGUST

S	M	T	W	T	F	S
				1	2	3
4	5	6	7	8	9	10
11	12	13	14	15	16	17
18	19	20	21	22	23	24
25	26	27	28	29	30	31

DECEMBER

S	M	T	W	T	F	S
1	2	3	4	5	6	7
8	9	10	11	12	13	14
15	16	17	18	19	20	21
22	23	24	25	26	27	28
29	30	31				

J

JANUARY

S	M	T	W	T	F	S
			1	2	3	4
5	6	7	8	9	10	11
12	13	14	15	16	17	18
19	20	21	22	23	24	25
26	27	28	29	30	31	

MAY

S	M	T	W	T	F	S
				1	2	3
4	5	6	7	8	9	10
11	12	13	14	15	16	17
18	19	20	21	22	23	24
25	26	27	28	29	30	31

SEPTEMBER

S	M	T	W	T	F	S
	1	2	3	4	5	6
7	8	9	10	11	12	13
14	15	16	17	18	19	20
21	22	23	24	25	26	27
28	29	30				

FEBRUARY

S	M	T	W	T	F	S
					1	2
3	4	5	6	7	8	9
10	11	12	13	14	15	16
17	18	19	20	21	22	23
24	25	26	27	28	29	

JUNE

S	M	T	W	T	F	S
1	2	3	4	5	6	7
8	9	10	11	12	13	14
15	16	17	18	19	20	21
22	23	24	25	26	27	28
29	30					

OCTOBER

S	M	T	W	T	F	S
			1	2	3	4
5	6	7	8	9	10	11
12	13	14	15	16	17	18
19	20	21	22	23	24	25
26	27	28	29	30	31	

MARCH

S	M	T	W	T	F	S
						1
2	3	4	5	6	7	8
9	10	11	12	13	14	15
16	17	18	19	20	21	22
23	24	25	26	27	28	29
30	31					

JULY

S	M	T	W	T	F	S
		1	2	3	4	5
6	7	8	9	10	11	12
13	14	15	16	17	18	19
20	21	22	23	24	25	26
27	28	29	30	31		

NOVEMBER

S	M	T	W	T	F	S
						1
2	3	4	5	6	7	8
9	10	11	12	13	14	15
16	17	18	19	20	21	22
23	24	25	26	27	28	29
30						

APRIL

S	M	T	W	T	F	S
		1	2	3	4	5
6	7	8	9	10	11	12
13	14	15	16	17	18	19
20	21	22	23	24	25	26
27	28	29	30			

AUGUST

S	M	T	W	T	F	S
					1	2
3	4	5	6	7	8	9
10	11	12	13	14	15	16
17	18	19	20	21	22	23
24	25	26	27	28	29	30
31						

DECEMBER

S	M	T	W	T	F	S
	1	2	3	4	5	6
7	8	9	10	11	12	13
14	15	16	17	18	19	20
21	22	23	24	25	26	27
28	29	30	31			

PERPETUAL CALENDAR

K

JANUARY	MAY	SEPTEMBER
S M T W T F S	S M T W T F S	S M T W T F S
1 2 3 4 5 6 7 8 9 10 11 12 13 14 15 16 17 18 19 20 21 22 23 24 25 26 27 28 29 30 31	1 2 3 4 5 6 7 8 9 10 11 12 13 14 15 16 17 18 19 20 21 22 23 24 25 26 27 28 29 30 31	1 2 3 4 5 6 7 8 9 10 11 12 13 14 15 16 17 18 19 20 21 22 23 24 25 26 27 28 29 30

FEBRUARY	JUNE	OCTOBER
S M T W T F S	S M T W T F S	S M T W T F S
1 2 3 4 5 6 7 8 9 10 11 12 13 14 15 16 17 18 19 20 21 22 23 24 25 26 27 28 29	1 2 3 4 5 6 7 8 9 10 11 12 13 14 15 16 17 18 19 20 21 22 23 24 25 26 27 28 29 30	1 2 3 4 5 6 7 8 9 10 11 12 13 14 15 16 17 18 19 20 21 22 23 24 25 26 27 28 29 30 31

MARCH	JULY	NOVEMBER
S M T W T F S	S M T W T F S	S M T W T F S
1 2 3 4 5 6 7 8 9 10 11 12 13 14 15 16 17 18 19 20 21 22 23 24 25 26 27 28 29 30 31	1 2 3 4 5 6 7 8 9 10 11 12 13 14 15 16 17 18 19 20 21 22 23 24 25 26 27 28 29 30 31	1 2 3 4 5 6 7 8 9 10 11 12 13 14 15 16 17 18 19 20 21 22 23 24 25 26 27 28 29 30

APRIL	AUGUST	DECEMBER
S M T W T F S	S M T W T F S	S M T W T F S
1 2 3 4 5 6 7 8 9 10 11 12 13 14 15 16 17 18 19 20 21 22 23 24 25 26 27 28 29 30	1 2 3 4 5 6 7 8 9 10 11 12 13 14 15 16 17 18 19 20 21 22 23 24 25 26 27 28 29 30 31	1 2 3 4 5 6 7 8 9 10 11 12 13 14 15 16 17 18 19 20 21 22 23 24 25 26 27 28 29 30 31

L

JANUARY	MAY	SEPTEMBER
S M T W T F S	S M T W T F S	S M T W T F S
1 2 3 4 5 6 7 8 9 10 11 12 13 14 15 16 17 18 19 20 21 22 23 24 25 26 27 28 29 30 31	1 2 3 4 5 6 7 8 9 10 11 12 13 14 15 16 17 18 19 20 21 22 23 24 25 26 27 28 29 30 31	1 2 3 4 5 6 7 8 9 10 11 12 13 14 15 16 17 18 19 20 21 22 23 24 25 26 27 28 29 30

FEBRUARY	JUNE	OCTOBER
S M T W T F S	S M T W T F S	S M T W T F S
1 2 3 4 5 6 7 8 9 10 11 12 13 14 15 16 17 18 19 20 21 22 23 24 25 26 27 28 29	1 2 3 4 5 6 7 8 9 10 11 12 13 14 15 16 17 18 19 20 21 22 23 24 25 26 27 28 29 30	1 2 3 4 5 6 7 8 9 10 11 12 13 14 15 16 17 18 19 20 21 22 23 24 25 26 27 28 29 30 31

MARCH	JULY	NOVEMBER
S M T W T F S	S M T W T F S	S M T W T F S
1 2 3 4 5 6 7 8 9 10 11 12 13 14 15 16 17 18 19 20 21 22 23 24 25 26 27 28 29 30 31	1 2 3 4 5 6 7 8 9 10 11 12 13 14 15 16 17 18 19 20 21 22 23 24 25 26 27 28 29 30 31	1 2 3 4 5 6 7 8 9 10 11 12 13 14 15 16 17 18 19 20 21 22 23 24 25 26 27 28 29 30

APRIL	AUGUST	DECEMBER
S M T W T F S	S M T W T F S	S M T W T F S
1 2 3 4 5 6 7 8 9 10 11 12 13 14 15 16 17 18 19 20 21 22 23 24 25 26 27 28 29 30	1 2 3 4 5 6 7 8 9 10 11 12 13 14 15 16 17 18 19 20 21 22 23 24 25 26 27 28 29 30 31	1 2 3 4 5 6 7 8 9 10 11 12 13 14 15 16 17 18 19 20 21 22 23 24 25 26 27 28 29 30 31

M

JANUARY
S	M	T	W	T	F	S
					1	2
3	4	5	6	7	8	9
10	11	12	13	14	15	16
17	18	19	20	21	22	23
24	25	26	27	28	29	30
31						

MAY
S	M	T	W	T	F	S
1	2	3	4	5	6	7
8	9	10	11	12	13	14
15	16	17	18	19	20	21
22	23	24	25	26	27	28
29	30	31				

SEPTEMBER
S	M	T	W	T	F	S
				1	2	3
4	5	6	7	8	9	10
11	12	13	14	15	16	17
18	19	20	21	22	23	24
25	26	27	28	29	30	

FEBRUARY
S	M	T	W	T	F	S
	1	2	3	4	5	6
7	8	9	10	11	12	13
14	15	16	17	18	19	20
21	22	23	24	25	26	27
28	29					

JUNE
S	M	T	W	T	F	S
			1	2	3	4
5	6	7	8	9	10	11
12	13	14	15	16	17	18
19	20	21	22	23	24	25
26	27	28	29	30		

OCTOBER
S	M	T	W	T	F	S
						1
2	3	4	5	6	7	8
9	10	11	12	13	14	15
16	17	18	19	20	21	22
23	24	25	26	27	28	29
30	31					

MARCH
S	M	T	W	T	F	S
	1	2	3	4	5	
6	7	8	9	10	11	12
13	14	15	16	17	18	19
20	21	22	23	24	25	26
27	28	29	30	31		

JULY
S	M	T	W	T	F	S
					1	2
3	4	5	6	7	8	9
10	11	12	13	14	15	16
17	18	19	20	21	22	23
24	25	26	27	28	29	30
31						

NOVEMBER
S	M	T	W	T	F	S
		1	2	3	4	5
6	7	8	9	10	11	12
13	14	15	16	17	18	19
20	21	22	23	24	25	26
27	28	29	30			

APRIL
S	M	T	W	T	F	S
					1	2
3	4	5	6	7	8	9
10	11	12	13	14	15	16
17	18	19	20	21	22	23
24	25	26	27	28	29	30

AUGUST
S	M	T	W	T	F	S
	1	2	3	4	5	6
7	8	9	10	11	12	13
14	15	16	17	18	19	20
21	22	23	24	25	26	27
28	29	30	31			

DECEMBER
S	M	T	W	T	F	S
				1	2	3
4	5	6	7	8	9	10
11	12	13	14	15	16	17
18	19	20	21	22	23	24
25	26	27	28	29	30	31

N

JANUARY
S	M	T	W	T	F	S
						1
2	3	4	5	6	7	8
9	10	11	12	13	14	15
16	17	18	19	20	21	22
23	24	25	26	27	28	29
30	31					

MAY
S	M	T	W	T	F	S
	1	2	3	4	5	6
7	8	9	10	11	12	13
14	15	16	17	18	19	20
21	22	23	24	25	26	27
28	29	30	31			

SEPTEMBER
S	M	T	W	T	F	S
					1	2
3	4	5	6	7	8	9
10	11	12	13	14	15	16
17	18	19	20	21	22	23
24	25	26	27	28	29	30

FEBRUARY
S	M	T	W	T	F	S
		1	2	3	4	5
6	7	8	9	10	11	12
13	14	15	16	17	18	19
20	21	22	23	24	25	26
27	28	29				

JUNE
S	M	T	W	T	F	S
				1	2	3
4	5	6	7	8	9	10
11	12	13	14	15	16	17
18	19	20	21	22	23	24
25	26	27	28	29	30	

OCTOBER
S	M	T	W	T	F	S
1	2	3	4	5	6	7
8	9	10	11	12	13	14
15	16	17	18	19	20	21
22	23	24	25	26	27	28
29	30	31				

MARCH
S	M	T	W	T	F	S
			1	2	3	4
5	6	7	8	9	10	11
12	13	14	15	16	17	18
19	20	21	22	23	24	25
26	27	28	29	30	31	

JULY
S	M	T	W	T	F	S
						1
2	3	4	5	6	7	8
9	10	11	12	13	14	15
16	17	18	19	20	21	22
23	24	25	26	27	28	29
30	31					

NOVEMBER
S	M	T	W	T	F	S
			1	2	3	4
5	6	7	8	9	10	11
12	13	14	15	16	17	18
19	20	21	22	23	24	25
26	27	28	29	30		

APRIL
S	M	T	W	T	F	S
						1
2	3	4	5	6	7	8
9	10	11	12	13	14	15
16	17	18	19	20	21	22
23	24	25	26	27	28	29
30						

AUGUST
S	M	T	W	T	F	S
		1	2	3	4	5
6	7	8	9	10	11	12
13	14	15	16	17	18	19
20	21	22	23	24	25	26
27	28	29	30	31		

DECEMBER
S	M	T	W	T	F	S
					1	2
3	4	5	6	7	8	9
10	11	12	13	14	15	16
17	18	19	20	21	22	23
24	25	26	27	28	29	30
31						

TABLE OF SQUARES CUBES, SQUARE ROOTS, AND CUBE ROOTS

No.	Square	Cube	Square Root	Cube Root
1	1	1	1.000	1.000
2	4	8	1.414	1.260
3	9	27	1.732	1.442
4	16	64	2.000	1.587
5	25	125	2.236	1.710
6	36	216	2.449	1.817
7	49	343	2.646	1.913
8	64	512	2.828	2.000
9	81	729	3.000	2.080
10	100	1,000	3.162	2.154
11	121	1,331	3.317	2.224
12	144	1,728	3.464	2.289
13	169	2,197	3.606	2.351
14	196	2,744	3.742	2.410
15	225	3,375	3.873	2.466
16	256	4,096	4.000	2.520
17	289	4,913	4.123	2.571
18	324	5,832	4.243	2.621
19	361	6,859	4.359	2.668
20	400	8,000	4.472	2.714
21	441	9,261	4.583	2.759
22	484	10,648	4.690	2.802
23	529	12,167	4.796	2.488

No.	Square	Cube	Square Root	Cube Root
24	576	13,824	4.899	2.884
25	625	15,625	5.000	2.924
26	676	17,576	5.099	2.962
27	729	19,683	5.196	3.000
28	784	21,952	5.292	3.037
29	841	24,389	5.385	3.072
30	900	27,000	5.477	3.107
31	961	29,791	5.568	3.141
32	1,024	32,768	5.657	3.175
33	1,089	35,937	5.745	3.208
34	1,156	39,304	5.831	3.240
35	1,225	42,875	5.916	3.271
36	1,296	46,656	6.000	3.302
37	1,369	50,653	6.083	3.332
38	1,444	54,872	6.164	3.362
39	1,521	59,319	6.245	3.391
40	1,600	64,000	6.325	3.420
41	1,681	68,921	6.403	3.448
42	1,764	74,088	6.481	3.476
43	1,849	79,507	6.557	3.503
44	1,936	85,184	6.633	3.530
45	2,025	91,125	6.708	3.557
46	2,116	97,336	6.782	3.583
47	2,209	103,823	6.856	3.609
48	2,304	110,592	6.928	3.634
49	2,401	117,649	7.000	3.659
50	2,500	125,000	7.071	3.684
51	2,601	132,651	7.141	3.708

TABLE OF SQUARE AND CUBE ROOTS

No.	Square	Cube	Square Root	Cube Root
52	2,704	140,608	7.211	3.732
53	2,809	148,877	7.208	3.756
54	2,916	157,464	7.348	3.780
55	3,025	166,375	7.416	3.803
56	3,136	175,616	7.483	3.826
57	3,249	185,193	7.550	3.848
58	3,364	195,112	7.616	3.871
59	3,481	205,379	7.681	3.893
60	3,600	216,000	7.746	3.915
61	3,721	226,981	7.810	3.936
62	3,844	238,328	7.874	3.958
63	3,969	250,047	7.937	3.979
64	4,096	262,144	8.000	4.000
65	4,225	274,625	8.062	4.021
66	4,356	287,496	8.124	4.041
67	4,489	300,763	8.185	4.061
68	4,624	314,432	8.246	4.082
69	4,761	328,509	8.307	4.101
70	4,900	343,000	8.367	4.121
71	5,041	357,911	8.426	4.141
72	5,184	373,248	8.485	4.160
73	5,329	389,017	8.544	4.179
74	5,476	405,224	8.602	4.198
75	5,625	421,875	8.660	4.217
76	5,776	438,976	8.718	4.236
77	5,929	456,533	8.775	4.254
78	6,084	474,552	8.832	4.273
79	6,241	493,039	8.888	4.291
80	6,400	512,000	8.944	4.309

No.	Square	Cube	Square Root	Cube Root
81	6,561	531,441	9.000	4.327
82	6,724	551,368	9.055	4.344
83	6,889	571,787	9.110	4.362
84	7,056	592,704	9.165	4.379
85	7,225	614,125	9.219	4.397
86	7,396	636,056	9.274	4.414
87	7,569	658,503	9.327	4.431
88	7,744	681,472	9.381	4.448
89	7,921	704,969	9.434	4.465
90	8,100	729,000	9.487	4.481
91	8,281	753,571	9.539	4.498
92	8,464	778,688	9.592	4.514
93	8,649	804,357	9.644	4.531
94	8,836	830,584	9.695	4.547
95	9,025	857,375	9.747	4.563
96	9,216	884,736	9.798	4.579
97	9,409	912,673	9.849	4.595
98	9,604	941,192	9.899	4.610
99	9,801	970,299	9.950	4.626
100	10,000	1,000,000	10.000	4.642

METRICATION TABLES

Conversion to Metric Units		Conversion from Metric Units	
LINEAR MEASURE (LENGTH)			
To convert	Multiply by	To convert	Multiply by
inches to millimeters	25.4	millimeters to inches	0.039
inches to centimeters	2.54	centimeters to inches	0.394
feet to meters	0.305	meters to feet	3.281
yards to meters	0.914	meters to yards	1.094
miles to kilometers	1.609	kilometers to miles	0.621
SQUARE MEASURE (AREA)			
To convert	Multiply by	To convert	Multiply by
sq. inches to sq. centimeters	6.452	sq. centimeters to sq. inches	0.155
sq. feet to sq. meters	0.093	sq. meters to sq. feet	10.764
sq. yards to sq. meters	0.836	sq. meters to sq. yards	1.196
acres to hectares	0.405	hectares to acres	2.471

METRICATION TABLES (Con't)

CUBIC MEASURE (VOLUME)

To convert	Multiply by
cu. inches to cu. centimeters	16.387
cu. feet to cu. meters	0.028
cu. yards to cu. meters	0.765

To convert	Multiply by
cu. centimeters to cu. inches	0.061
cu. meters to cu. feet	35.315
cu. meters to cu. yards	1.308

LIQUID MEASURE (CAPACITY)

To convert	Multiply by
fluid ounces to liters	0.03
quarts to liters	0.946
gallons to liters	3.785
imperial gallons to liters	4.546

To convert	Multiply by
liters to fluid ounces	33.814
liters to quarts	1.057
liters to gallons	0.264
liters to imperial gallons	0.220

WEIGHTS (MASS)

To convert	Multiply by
ounces avoirdupois to grams	28.35
pounds avoirdupois to kilograms	0.454
tons to metric tons	0.907

To convert	Multiply by
grams to ounces avoirdupois	0.035
kilograms to pounds avoirdupois	2.205
metric tons to tons	1.102

METRICATION TABLES

TEMPERATURE

Fahrenheit thermometer   **Celsius (or Centigrade) thermometer**

32°F	freezing point of water	0°C
212°F	boiling point of water	100°C
98.6°F	body temperature	37°C

To find degrees Celsius, subtract 32 from degrees Fahrenheit and divide by 1.8.
To find degrees Fahrenheit, multiply degrees Celsius by 1.8 and add 32.

TABLES OF WEIGHTS AND MEASURES

Linear Measure

1 mil = 0.001 inch	=	0.0254	millimeter
1 inch = 1.000 mils	=	2.54	centimeters

181

Tables of Weights and Measures (Con't)

12 inches	= 1 foot	= 0.3048 meter
3 feet	= 1 yard	= 0.9144 meter
5½ yards or 16½ feet	= 1 rod (or pole or perch)	= 5.029 meters
40 rods	= 1 furlong	= 201.168 meters
8 furlongs or 1,760 yards or 5,280 feet	= 1 (statute) mile	= 1.6093 kilometers
3 miles	= 1 (land) league	= 4.83 kilometers

Square Measure

	1 square inch	= 6.452 square centimeters
144 square inches	= 1 square foot	= 929.03 square centimeters
9 square feet	= 1 square yard	= 0.8361 square meter
30¼ square yards	= 1 square rod (or square pole or square perch)	= 25.292 square meters
160 square rods or 4,840 square yards or 43,560 square feet	= 1 acre	= 0.4047 hectare
640 acres	= 1 square mile	= 259.00 hectares or 2.590 square kilometers

TABLES OF WEIGHTS AND MEASURES

Cubic Measure

| 1,728 cubic inches | = | 1 cubic inch = 16.387 cubic centimeters |
| | | 1 cubic foot = 0.0283 cubic meter |

27 cubic feet = 1 cubic yard = 0.7646 cubic meter
(in units for cordwood, etc.)

16 cubic feet = 1 cord foot = 0.453 cubic meter
128 cubic feet = 1 cord = 3.625 cubic meters

or

8 cord feet

Nautical Measure

6 feet = 1 fathom = 1.829 meters

100 fathoms = 1 cable's length (ordinary)
(In the U.S. Navy 120 fathoms or 720 feet, or 219.456 meters) = 1 cable's length
(In the British Navy, 608 feet, or 185.319 meters) = 1 cable's length

10 cable's length = 1 international nautical mile = 1.852 kilometers (exactly)
(6,076.11549 feet, by international agreement)

1 international nautical mile = 1.150779 statute miles (the length of a minute of longitude at the equator)

3 nautical miles = 1 marine league (3.45 statute miles) = 5.56 kilometers

60 nautical miles = 1 degree of a great circle of the earth = 69.047 statute miles

HANDBOOK OF PRACTICAL INFORMATION

Tables of Weights and Measures (Con't)

Dry Measure

	1 pint	=	33.60 cubic inches = 0.5506 liter
2 pints	= 1 quart	=	67.20 cubic inches = 1.1012 liter
8 quarts	= 1 peck	=	537.61 cubic inches = 8.8098 liter
4 pecks	= 1 bushel	=	2,150.42 cubic inches = 35.2390 liters

According to U.S. standards, following are the weights avoirdupois for single bushels of the specified grains: for wheat, 60 pounds; for barley, 48 pounds; for oats, 32 pounds; for rye, 56 pounds; for shelled corn, 56 pounds. Some States have specifications varying from these. The British dry quart = 1.032 U.S. dry quarts

Dry Measure

Liquid Measure

1 gill	= 4 fluid ounces =	7.219 cubic inches = 0.1183 liter
	(see next table)	
4 gills	= 1 pint	= 28.875 cubic inches = 0.4732 liter
2 pints	= 1 quart	= 57.75 cubic inches = 0.9464 liter
4 quarts	= 1 gallon	= 231 cubic inches = 3.7854 liters

The British imperial gallon (4 imperial quarts) = 277.42 cubic inches = 4.546 liters. The barrel in Great Britain equals 36 imperial gallons, in the United States, usually 31½ gallons.

Apothecaries' Fluid Measure

	1 minim	= 0.0038 cubic inch	= 0.0616 milliliter
60 minims	= 1 fluid dram	= 0.2256 cubic inch	= 3.6966 milliliters
8 fluid drams	= 1 fluid ounce	= 1.8047 cubic inches	= 0.0296 liter
16 fluid ounces	= 1 pint	= 28.875 cubic inches	= 0.4732 liter

See table immediately preceding for quart and gallon equivalents.
The British pint = 20 fluid ounces.

Tables of Weights and Measures (Con't)

Circular (or Angular) Measure

60 seconds (")	= 1 minute (')
60 minutes	= 1 degree (°)
90 degrees	= 1 quadrant or 1 right angle
180 degrees	= 2 quadrants or 1 straight angle
4 quadrants or 360 degrees	= 1 circle

Tables of Weights and Measures (Con't)

Avoirdupois Weight

(The grain, equal to 0.0648 gram, is the same in all three tables of weight.)

1 dram or 27.34 grains	= 1.772	grams
16 drams or 437.5 grains = 1 ounce	= 28.3495	grams
16 ounces or 7,000 grains = 1 pound	= 453.59	grams
100 pounds = 1 hundredweight	= 45.36	kilograms
2,000 pounds = 1 ton	= 907.18	kilograms

In Great Britain, 14 pounds (6.35 kilograms) = 1 stone, 112 pounds (50.80 kilograms) = 1 hundredweight, and 2,240 pounds (1,016.05 kilograms) = 1 long ton.

Troy Weight

(The grain, equal to 0.0648 gram, is the same in all three tables or weight.)

3.086 grains = 1 carat	= 200.00	milligrams
24 grains = 1 pennyweight	= 1.5552	grams
20 pennyweights or 480 grains = 1 ounce	= 31.1035	grams
12 ounces or 5,760 grains = 1 pound	= 373.24	grams

TABLES OF WEIGHTS AND MEASURES

Apothecaries' Weight

(The grain, equal to 0.0648 gram, is the same in all three tables of weight.)

20 grains	= 1 scruple	1.296 grams
3 scruples	= 1 dram	3.888 grams
8 drams or 480 grains	= 1 ounce	31.1035 grams
12 ounces or 5,760 grains	= 1 pound	373.24 grams

THE METRIC SYSTEM
Linear Measure

1 millimeter	=	0.03937 inch
10 millimeters = 1 centimeter	=	0.3937 inch
10 centimeters = 1 decimeter	=	3.937 inches
10 decimeters = 1 meter	=	39.37 inches
10 meters = 1 decameter	=	393.7 inches or 3.2808 feet

Tables of Weights and Measures (Con't)

10 decameters = 1 hectometer =	328.08	feet
10 hectometers = 1 kilometer =	0.621	mile or 3,280.8 feet
10 kilometers = 1 myriameter =	6.21	miles

Square Measure

1 square millimeter =	0.00155	square inch
100 square millimeters = 1 square centimeter =	0.15499	square inch
100 square centimeters = 1 square decimeter =	15.499	square inches
100 square decimeters = 1 square meter =	1,549.9	square inches or 1.196 square yards
100 square meters = 1 square decameter =	119.6	square yards
100 square decameters = 1 square hectometer =	2.471	acres
100 square hectometers = 1 square kilometer =	0.386	square mile or 247.1 acres

Land Measure

1 square meter = 1 centiare =	1,549.9	square inches
100 centiares = 1 are =	119.6	square yards
100 ares = 1 hectare =	2.471	acres
100 hectares = 1 square kilometer =	0.386	square mile or 247.1 acres

TABLES OF WEIGHTS AND MEASURES

Volume Measure

1,000 cubic millimeters = 1 cubic centimeter = 0.06102 cubic inch
1,000 cubic centimeters = 1 cubic decimeter = 61.023 cubic inches or 0.0353 cubic foot
1,000 cubic decimeters = 1 cubic meter = 35.314 cubic feet or 1.308 cubic yards

Capacity Measure

10 milliliters = 1 centiliter =	0.338	fluid ounce
10 centiliters = 1 deciliter =	3.38	fluid ounces or 0.1057 liquid quart
10 deciliters = 1 liter =	1.0567	liquid quarts or 0.9081 dry quart
10 liters = 1 decaliter =	2.64	gallons or 0.284 bushel
10 decaliters = 1 hectoliter =	26.418	gallons or 2.838 bushels
10 hectoliters = 1 kiloliter =	264.18	gallons or 35.315 cubic feet

Weights

10 milligrams = 1 centigram =	0.1543	grain or 0.000353 ounce (avdp.)
10 centigrams = 1 decigram =	1.5432	grains
10 decigrams = 1 gram =	15.432	grains or 0.035274 ounce (avdp.)
10 grams = 1 decagram =	0.3527	ounce
10 decagrams = 1 hectogram =	3.5274	ounces
10 hectograms = 1 kilogram =	2.2046	pounds
10 kilograms = 1 myriagram =	22.046	pounds
10 myriagrams = 1 quintal =	220.46	pounds
10 quintals = 1 metric ton =	2,204.6	pounds

FAMILY LEGAL GUIDE

FAMILY LEGAL GUIDE
TABLE OF CONTENTS

FAMILY
LEGAL GUIDE
Introduction

This book is not a law text nor is it a how-to manual on practicing law. Instead it is an informative guide about the laws that affect you and your family as you go about your daily business and personal activities. It is a guide to help you understand and recognize common legal problems and methods of dealing with them.

In general, the purpose of laws is to protect the rights of individuals but also to protect the rights of society — the overall group, the people we are a part of. However, although law protects the rights of the individual, to a large degree our legal system depends on the individual to protect himself — to know both what his rights and his obligations are. As has been said many times, "Ignorance is no excuse."

The purpose of this section, then, is to provide you with useful guidelines and information concerning the basic legal rules which govern personal injuries, property damage, property purchase and sale, leases, employee rights, executing a will, contracts, family disputes include divorce and child custody, and more.

The information presented here is not meant to be a substitute for a lawyer. Instead it is intended to enable you to understand certain situations where legal rules apply before any problems or disputes arise.

There are times when the use of a lawyer's services are absolutely essential or desirable. In fact, if you do not obtain competent legal counsel when needed, you are losing the opportunity to use law and the legal system to defend and secure your rights. You should know and understand when you do need a lawyer, how to secure the right kind of lawyer, and then how to work with the lawyer and make most effective use of his services.

Chapter 1
YOU AND THE LAW

Basically, law is a system of rules and a standard of conduct that has been developed or designed for the common good. This good is for the individual but also for the good of society as a whole.

Law both protects our rights as well as requiring us to do or to refrain from doing certain things. In many ways, it affects or governs almost all of our daily activities or actions. It requires the registration of our birth and supervises the distribution of our possessions upon our death. It requires our children to go to school until a certain age and restricts the speed and the manner in which we drive.

The law sets forth requirements for our marriage and what must be done if the marriage is to be dissolved. It stipulates methods of business conduct and protects us from unfair or deceptive business practices. It provides recompense if we are injured and penalties if we should injure someone else. There is almost no limit to the way in which law affects our lives.

Your Rights

In the United States, the law is based on the Constitution and the preservation of Constitutional rights. Under the Constitution you have certain obligations or duties, but you also have certain rights which are protected. Some of the more important guaranteed rights are:

1) Freedom of speech and the press

2) Freedom of assembly and religion

3) The right to vote and to hold public office

4) Equal protection under the laws

5) Protection of individual privacy

6) Full enjoyment of one's property

7)   Due process of law

Laws are designed to protect the individual's rights or interests provided no one else is harmed, plus, of course, to protect society's rights. There are two basic principles under which the law operates:

1)   *Fairness* — If a wrong has been committed, the remedy should, as much as possible, make amends for the wrong.

2)   *Equality* — All individuals, without exception, are to be treated alike under the law.

Although change is slow, the Constitution grows and changes constantly. From time to time there are written additions, but most of the change occurs through interpretation by court decisions — principally Supreme Court decisions. The rights defined by the Constitution and court decisions fall into two main groups, substantive and procedural rights.

Substantive Rights
Substantive rights are those rights which have important basic, intrinsic value to the individual — rights like freedom of speech and religion, and protection of one's right of privacy and one's property. However, if a person's act violates the rights of others or is contrary to a law, the act becomes illegal even though, theoretically, it is the exercise of a substantive right.

Procedural Rights
Procedural rights are those that provide that no one will be convicted of a crime or violation unless evidence has been fairly presented and judged impartially. For example, a defendant in a criminal trial has the right to have counsel and also the right to trial by a jury. In addition, illegal searches

of a house or other property and the illegal seizure of papers or other items is prohibited.. The Fifth Amendment of the Constitution provides that no person can be "deprived of life, liberty or property, without the process of law... ." All states have laws which give special protection to minors both in criminal and non-criminal cases.

Types of Law*

There are federal, state, and local laws. These laws can, in turn, be classified as to whether they pertain to civil or criminal law. In civil law the injured party is another individual. In criminal law, society is considered to be the injured party although the crime may also have injured an individual.

Civil law and civil suits may involve any of the following:

1) Contract enforcement or violation

2) Automobile or other accidents

3) Injuries on the job or elsewhere

4) Family disputes — divorce, child custody, etc.

5) Injuries to one's reputation

6) Wills and estates

7) Violation of personal rights

8) Property rights — violation or damage

Criminal law is concerned with offenses that are considered serious enough to be regarded as offenses against society. In criminal cases, the state or federal government is the party bringing suit rather than an individual. Various states have somewhat different laws, but the most common or important crimes are:

---

* See Canadian Law, page 94.

Murder	Kidnapping
Voluntary manslaughter	Criminal negligence
Rape	Larceny
Robbery	Embezzlement
Burglary	Forgery
Assault and Battery	Receiving stolen goods
Arson	Accessory to a crime

Violations of local ordinances such as traffic laws, building codes, etc. are generally not regarded as crimes although they are violations of a law. Such violations can bring a fine or other penalty.

The Court System

A court is used to settle disputes between individuals and to provide a means for the enforcement of criminal law. There is a state system and a federal system.

State courts determine the majority of suits or questions concerning contracts, personal injuries, family disputes, wills, and crime. Federal courts determine questions concerning the U.S. Constitution, federal laws, disputes between states, and civil suits involving citizens of different states.

Although they are not courts, there are a large number of administrative governmental agencies that control, interpret, or enforce various laws or regulations. These agencies are concerned with banking, insurance, public utilities, motor vehicles, taxation, and the regulation and licensing of professions and occupations.

Both the federal and state court systems have courts of original jurisdiction and courts of appeal. The original court is also known as the trial court. It is in this court that a civil or criminal proceeding is started and the original ruling or decision is made.

However, if the loser of a trial believes that certain substantive or procedural laws were violated during the trial, he can appeal to a court of appellate jurisdiction. The appellate court reviews the trial court's decision and rules whether or not the decision should be upheld or reversed.

Rights to a Jury

In most states if the individual desires it, he usually can have civil cases heard before a jury. If the individual wishes it, or in states that do not provide for a jury, a judge will hear and determine the case alone.

In a state criminal case, a judge and a jury determine whether the state has proven the criminal charges beyond a reasonable doubt. If not, the defendant is acquitted. However, a criminal defendant also can waive his right to a jury trial and appear solely before a judge.

The preceeding has described the basic framework within which the law operates. The remaining sections examine specific areas of the law and some of the practical legal problems that may arise in your daily activities.

Chapter 2
PERSONAL AND PROPERTY INJURIES

Laws and courts everywhere recognize that whenever possible and to the degree possible the courts should compensate persons who are harmed by the actions or negligence of others. One of the most common examples is the automobile accident.

Negligence actions, however, are not limited to automobile cases. They include cases involving improperly guarded or defective equipment, defective goods or merchandise, malpractice of medical personnel, falling or tripping on a person's property, in fact, from any sort of accident or event that causes *either a mental or physical injury*. A person may be liable for such offenses as assault, trespass, defamation of character, libel, and others.

Tort Law

The law of negligence falls under what is called *tort law*. Tort law is based on the theory that anyone who causes injury or harm to another person or a person's property is responsible for the harm whether or not caused by negligence or intent. Tort law is different than criminal law. Under criminal law, the offense is against society, and the state imposes punishment on the guilty party. Tort law also differs from contract law which legally enforces the promises or obligations of various persons or groups.

A tort is a civil wrong and is the violation of a personal right that has been guaranteed to a person by law. A tort is committed if a person interferes with another person's liberty, safety, health, reputation, or his private property. If a person claims injury and can prove it, the court will hold the defendant responsible and will assess a penalty.

Kinds of Tort Liability

An individual can easily become involved in a liability situation, often through little or no direct fault of his own. You, therefore, should know what actions might create a liability on your part, and what your rights are or what action you should take if an accident or injury occurs to you. It is legitimate to enforce your rights when you are genuinely injured through the negligence or actions of another.

Personal liability can be divided into three broad areas:

1) Liability as a result of intentional conduct;

2) Liability as a result of negligent conduct;

3) Liability without fault.

An injury to a person's body is referred to as *personal injury* or *bodily injury,* and can be either physical or mental. *Property damage* may be the result of a car accident or damage to a building, house, and so on.

Intentional Conduct Liability

If a person knowingly violates the rights of another, he has committed an intentional tort. Intentional tort includes a wide variety of actions including assault and battery, trespass, fraud, conversion, false arrest, and others. To collect damages, you, as the victim, must generally prove that the act was done with malicious intent. The damages you collect, however, may be both actual and punitive to compensate for "pain and suffering."

Assault and Battery

Assault is an intentional act which creates a reasonable fear or apprehension that the aggressor intends and is able to harm a person. There need be only a threat of physical harm without any actual contact. Assault damages may be recoverable for fright or mental distress.

Threatening with a club, pitch fork, gun, or other weapon, even if there is no touching or contact, is an assault. The aggressor must have some ability to carry out injury or harm. Usually there must be some overt act such as threatening with a club or weapon. However, abusive tactics by a collection agency have been ruled by courts to be deliberate infliction of fear and mental suffering.

Battery is a completed assault; that is, there is actual physical contact or touching. If a person is hit with a club, a fist, or shot with a gun, battery has been committed.

Battery may also occur as the result of an unauthorized surgical operation, one for which the patient has not signed a legal consent. Doctors who touch their patients unnecessarily may be liable for battery. A person who commits a battery may, of course, also be subject to criminal proceedings and subject to fines and imprisonment by society in addition to his liability to the person injured.

Trespass

A trespass is an unlawful invasion of another's real property. The trespass sometimes may be unintentional, but even so, damages may be collectable. Trespass may simply be using someone else's property as a shortcut. Or it may be someone building on your property, children throwing stones at your house, someone causing a fire on your property because of some action, and a myriad of other things that cause damage. Damages caused by flowing water, sewage or other pollution, and offensive odors have been ruled as trespass.

Conversion

Trespass applies to invasion of real property. Conversion refers to taking or appropriating someone else's personal property, either openly or fraudulently, and altering it, misusing it, or converting it to your own use. Personal property includes tangible possessions such as jewelry, cars, appliances, etc., or intangible property such as stocks or bonds.

Examples of conversion: a mechanic taking a car that has been left for repair and driving it around for his own use; a cleaner dyeing a dress purple when it was left only for cleaning; taking and using your neighbor's lawnmower without his permission; convincing someone to give you money as an investment when there is no legitimate or actual investment venture. The later would be fraud but is also conversion.

False Arrest or Imprisonment
False imprisonment is a violation of the individual's right of personal liberty; that is, it is unlawful restraint. It would occur if you were illegally put in jail. It might also occur if a person was suspected of shoplifting and detained in a locked space by the store. However, shoplifting has become such a major problem that many states have modified their laws so that a person may be detained if there is reasonable belief that he has stolen merchandise.

False arrest is maliciously causing a person to be unlawfully arrested. If the person were also unlawfully imprisoned the two charges would be combined and subject to damages.

Negligent Conduct Liability

Negligence cases are by far the most common form of tort suit largely because automobile accident cases come under this head. It is important that you know the rules of legal liability so that you know whether the other person is liable to you, or you to him.

In order to sustain a liability action, a person's conduct must be negligent. This means conduct which falls below a reasonable standard — the standard of care the law considers you owe to others. The prerequisites of a successful negligence suit are these:

1)   There is a *duty* to use reasonable care and give proper
     attention in a certain situation;

2)   There is *conduct* which lacks the reasonable care and
     diligence that could be expected under the circumstances;

3)   There is a reasonably close *relationship* between the cause
     and effect;

4)   There is *no legal defense* to the action;

5)   There is *damage* as a result of the action.

Kinds of Negligence

Since we are dealing with humans and human conduct, there
are innumerable opportunities for negligence. Medical malpractice is the negligence of a doctor, dentist, or nurse to
follow generally accepted professional practices, care, or procedures. A factory owner may be negligent for not keeping
equipment in proper repair or because noxious fumes from the
factory are polluting the nearby area. A homeowner may be
liable because his unprotected swimming pool is an attractive
nuisance to neighborhood children. Negligent conduct can be
divided into the following general areas:

Harm Directly Caused by a Negligent Act

Any individual who fails to use reasonable care and caution
while performing a certain act is negligent. If a person improperly operates a car, does not use a reasonable amount of
care, violates traffic ordinances, etc., he is negligent. If a
doctor does not follow accepted practices or procedures and
the patient suffers injury, "pain or suffering," the doctor may
be guilty of malpractice — negligence. If a plumber fails to

properly install a hot water heater and as a result the basement is flooded, he is negligent.

Harm Caused By A Failure to Act

A person may be liable for injuries or damage if he has a duty to act or do something and he fails to do so. A homeowner or building owner who fails to keep a walkway free of ice and snow or to repair broken steps, may be negligent. Hotels, railroads, airlines, etc. have a duty to act in situations involving the public. If the person becomes ill or injured, the hotel, etc. must offer or secure help or be held liable for damages caused by aggravation of the illness. Business or industrial firms may be liable for damages if they fail to provide proper working conditions or protection for their employees or others.

Defective Goods or Machines

More and more today, manufacturers and sellers can be and are held liable for injury from defective goods or machines. This liability may be for: 1) negligence as already explained, 2) for breach of implied warranty, or 3) for liability under the general theory that a consumer has a right not to be injured if he uses a product according to instructions and in the normally intended manner.

Typically, sellers and producers can be sued for injury from products whose labels or instructions fail to properly inform consumers of the potential hazards of improper use. This lack of notice would be negligence. However, the potential for liability goes further than that. Manufacturers have and are being sued where a poison was introduced into a headache remedy; where razor blades or needles were found in candy; where glass or other foreign objects were found in baby food, soft drinks, soup, or other food; where an automobile part fails or responds inadequately under certain conditions thus causing an accident.

211

Millions of dollars worth of products have been recalled from store shelves because poison or foreign objects have been found in the product, often in isolated, localized cases. Toys have been recalled where there is a potential that a baby might swallow a part. Thousands of cars have been recalled for modification or replacement of a part because the manufacturer fears legal liability and in many cases has already been sued.

Manufacturers, of course, defend themselves and their products by claiming their product was not properly used, that instructions were not followed, that warnings were not heeded, that the product has been altered or tampered with perhaps by a third party, or for other reasons. However, the trend of court cases in this area has been in favor of consumers. Even though manufacturers have not been held negligent in the usual sense of the term, they have been held liable for injury caused by their product.

Changes in laws or court cases concerning product liability have substantially improved the lot of the consumer. No longer is it the rule of *caveat emptor* — let the buyer beware. In case of injury by a product, the best procedure is to sue everyone that has a significant relationship to the case — the manufacturer, the distributor, the seller, the installer. By doing so, anyone who may have contributed to or caused the injury is included.

No-fault Liability*

Previous sections presented information on intentional or negligent conduct which causes harm. There are areas where there is legal liability without fault. These are situations where neither party has intentionally interfered with another's person or property and both parties may have followed reasonable standards of care.

Certain activities are abnormally dangerous or hazardous.

* See Canadian Law, page 94.

Dynamite blasting is an example. If a construction company uses explosives and causes damage to adjoining property or even several blocks away, they may be liable. Common carriers or manufacturers of explosives, poison gases, or other dangerous materials have the same potential liability.

Dram shop laws have been passed in many states which hold sellers of intoxicants responsible for any injuries to another person that result from the intoxication of a customer. More recently, more and more cases or laws hold a homeowner or business host liable for injuries caused by guests or employees who have been served intoxicating liquor in the home, at an office party, etc.

Two situations where negligence suits are common are automobile accidents and work-related accidents. Because of their frequency and impact on those involved, special statutes have been passed to treat these cases on a "no-fault" basis.

No-fault Automobile Liability

Many states have passed statutes which do not take into account whose fault it was that caused the accident. These no-fault statutes provide that persons injured in an automobile accident are to be reimbursed for medical expenses or lost income by their own insurance company, regardless of who was responsible for the accident. *However, victims cannot recover from their own insurer for pain and suffering.*

Most states that have enacted no-fault laws have retained provisions for law suits to recover additional damages if you qualify. The circumstances under which you can still sue for pain and suffering are when there are serious injuries, such as the loss of a limb or if medical expenses exceed a specified dollar amount.

Where negligence suits are permitted, the action would be the same as taken against any party whose conduct has been negligent or in violation of any statutes. There are usually provisions for victims to sue reckless drivers or those under the influence of alcohol or drugs. There are also provisions giving protection coverage by the car owner's policy to passengers and to pedestrians struck by the car.

Workmen's Compensation

All states have workmen's compensation laws whereby the worker does not need to show that the employer was negligent. Work-related injuries subject to compensation include permanent or temporary disability, total or partial loss of use of various body parts, other permanent disabilities, and occupational diseases. However, the coverage is largely limited to medical expenses, loss of income, and sometimes recompense for disfigurement. The employer cannot be sued for "pain and suffering."

As a result, there is often an attempt to find a third party who can be sued for pain and suffering; for example, a manufacturer could be sued if it could be shown that a machine had a defect. An elevator maintenance company might be subject to liability if an elevator cable breaks. Third party suits, then, sometimes provide an opportunity for suits for pain and suffering where the employer cannot be sued under compensation laws.

Protecting Yourself

Whether you are at fault or not, you may commit a tort and be sued. You should have adequate insurance to protect yourself. Automobile liability is essential if you own a car and most states require such insurance. Every homeowner and tenant should have insurance, not only against fire and theft, but also against liability to persons who may fall down stairs, trip over furniture or rugs, slip on an icy sidewalk, or become intoxicated in your home and then injure himself or someone else.

The amount of insurance you carry should be determined by your means. Protection against all kinds of legal liability is highly desirable. There are "catastrophic" type insurance policies that, over and above your regular insurance, will protect you, at low cost, against almost all legal liability including legal expenses.

If you are sued for legal liability or receive a claim letter and are insured, you should notify your insurance company in writing at once. Write directly to the insurer, not to an agent. Send your letter by certified mail, return receipt requested. Enclose any letters, summons, etc. that you may have received. Keep copies of everything you send. If you are ever in an accident or aware of an accident or event for which you might be charged, notify the insurance company of the details at once. All liability policies contain provisions that require prompt notification of accident incidents or claims.

Once you have notified your insurer of a claim, he takes over the full defense of your case. The insurer hires the lawyer and pays all legal fees or other expenses. If there is a settlement, the insurer pays the settlement amount. After you have notified the insurer of the claim, you may hear little further about the case unless it goes to court.

If you are not insured, engage and consult with a lawyer at once. Or, if you have a policy but the insurer denies coverage, write and insist that they defend you. They may then do so leaving the question of whether they do or do not have liability to a later determination by a court or by an agreement with you. If they still refuse, engage your own lawyer. He may be able to convince the insurer to defend you. If not, you will need his services and advice to fight the case against you. You may or may not wish to sue the insurer at a later date.

What to Do If You Are Injured

If you are injured through the negligence of someone, it is legitimate to enforce your rights and seek compensation. Do not consider a suit for fairly trivial matters. However, if you are substantially injured, do not simply accept the injury or damage. Consult a competent attorney and discuss with him as to whether or not you have a good case. If he does not feel you should proceed, determine why. You must then determine whether to go ahead or not.

Personal-injury attorneys typically work on a contingent fee basis. In other words, they receive a percentage of the damages awarded and paid — usually thirty-three and a third percent but larger or lower fees may be negotiated or charged. Expenses of the case, such as court costs or expert witness fees, are deducted from the award before computing the lawyer's contingent fee.

If You Have An Accident

In most situations involving an accident (a tort liability), the incident happens quickly and the parties act or speak on impulse or with little thought. Protect your legal rights. Do not apologize or admit or state that you were wrong or made a mistake. Doing so can be highly detrimental to your case later on.

If you are in shock, physically injured, bleeding or in pain, you are not apt to evaluate the situation properly or assemble your thoughts normally. You may not fully appreciate or understand what really happened. Answer routine questions that the police or medical personnel ask you, otherwise largely keep quiet, making no admissions. Accept medical help at the scene of the accident and secure additional medical help and advice as soon as possible if there is any apparent or possible injury.

If you are involved in an accident, secure the following information as much as possible:

1) Date and time of the incident;

2) Exact place of the incident;

3) The names, addresses, and phone numbers of the driver of the other car, all passengers, and all witnesses;

4) License numbers, makes, and years of all cars;

5) Name of other driver's insurer and policy number;

6) Weather conditions if applicable;

7) Pictures if relevant and possible;

8) Name and address of any attending physician;

9) Notes of any statements made by witnesses or participants;

10) As soon as possible, make a brief written summary of all the facts and events.

If you feel you are the injured party, engage a competent negligence trial lawyer so that he can start his investigation immediately. The accident report should also be filed immediately with the proper municipal authorities and insurers. Inform your lawyer of everything. Do not discuss the accident with a stranger or the claim investigator from the wrongdoer's insurance company without clearing it with your attorney.

Follow your doctor's advice. Do not let the insurance company's doctor examine you without your lawyer's approval or attendance. Either to the insurer's doctor or others, do not give information without your lawyer's clearance. Follow his advice.

Chapter 3
CONTRACTS

In general, a contract is a promise which creates a legal obligation. Most of us enter into contracts every day, but we usually do not think of many of them in that way. If we subscribe to a magazine, we have entered into a contract. If we agree to buy a new car, we sign a paper which binds us to pay for the purchase. If you call the local department store and say ship me a certain television set and charge my account, you have made a contract.

Elements of A Contract

Essentially, a contract is a promise that can be enforced in a court of law. A contract may be oral, written, or implied. Legally, a contract requires an offer, an acceptance, and consideration.

The Offer:

An offer is a promise to do or not do something. The person who makes the offer is the "offeror." The person to whom it is made is the "offeree." The offer is conditioned upon acceptance by the offeree. The essential terms of the offer must be stated and must be communicated to the offeree. He must be aware of it.

To be valid, the terms of the offer must definitely be stated. If the terms are too indefinite, there can be no acceptance. An offer is not valid forever. It may be withdrawn before someone accepts provided the offeree is notified of the withdrawal. Usually the offer expires within a reasonable time, normally three months. Or if a time limit is stated in the original offer, it would expire at that time. The offer would also expire on the death of the offeror.

Acceptance:

An acceptance is an expression by the offeree that he agrees to the offer. This expression or consent can be accomplished by word or by deed. Silence never constitutes an acceptance. For example, if the offeror stated in his original offer, "If I do not hear from you, I will assume you have accepted," silence would not constitute acceptance. The acceptance must specifically be communicated to the offeror in some way. If the acceptance is mailed, sent by wire, etc., the acceptance of the offer is valid at the time the acceptance is deposited or sent, not when the assent is received by the offeror.

Consideration:

Consideration is what the parties do, give, or promise to do for each other. It is the inducement for the contracting party to enter into the contract. Consideration may be money, an object, an act, or forbearance from an act.

According to law, consideration must have two essential elements: 1) it must have value, and 2) it must be bargained for and given in return for the promise made. If a promise is made and nothing is given in return, there is no enforceable contract. If someone says, "I promise to give you $500," and you do not have to do anything for the $500, there is no contract.

The preceding sets forth the basic elements of contract law, which is perhaps the most important in the civil branch of American law. There can be many ramifications as to what was offered, what was intended, and what was accepted. However, the principles or essential elements remain the same.

The requirement that consideration have value, does not mean that it has to be a fair bargain or return. The law guarantees a person's right to contract for whatever terms he desires. The law is not permitted to void a contract just to make it fair (unless it is unconscionable) in their opinion. Many contracts say "in consideration of $1.00 and other valuable considerations.'' Normally, the law will uphold such contracts no matter what it is exchanged for.

Types of Contracts

Contracts may be written or oral, expressed or implied.

Oral Contracts:

Many people believe that an oral agreement is not valid. This is not true. Most oral contracts are enforceable and valid. Their main disadvantage is that they are difficult to prove. However, if you have one or more reliable witnesses that can testify to the contract, or other evidence, it may be enforceable.

Contracts That Must Be in Writing:*

Under the statute of frauds, there are some contracts that are not enforceable unless they are written. If a contract is of a certain kind, it does not matter that you have several witnesses that can testify that they heard the oral agreement being made. The courts must throw the case out if the contract is not written. The following contracts must be written:

1) *Contracts for the sale or leasing of land.* (Real estate transactions.)

2) *Contracts over an extended period.* (Any contract that cannot be fulfilled within one year — three years in some states — or within the promisor's lifetime.)

3) *Contracts to guarantee payment of a debt.* (Agreements to pay the debts of another, including an executor's or administrator's agreement to personally pay the debts of a decedent.)

4) *Contracts for sale of goods worth $500 or more.* (It must be signed by the person against whom the enforcement is to be made, unless the purchaser accepts delivery or

* See Canadian Law, page 95.

pays for all or part of the items when the agreement is reached.)

5) *Promises to make a will or trust.* (There must be a consideration.)

6) *Pre-nuptial agreements.* (A promise of something upon the marriage, or promises of something if the marriage is dissolved by death or otherwise.)

There are other agreements that require written confirmation. A written contract gives solid assurance as to what each of the two parties intended and is obligated to do. However, such assurance can sometimes be given other than in written form.

Unenforceable Contracts:*

Contracts entered into by a minor are usually not enforceable and can be disavowed by the minor at any time until he comes of age. This age varies from 18 to 21 in the various states. If the contract continues in force after that age, the minor is presumed to have affirmed the contract as an adult and then is bound by it. Minors who leave home and are not supported by their parents are "emancipated" and usually can be held to contracts for necessities such as food, clothing, housing, and medical expenses.

Mental incompetents cannot be held to a contract except for necessities unless their legal guardian affirms the contract. Contracts by minors can be guaranteed by an adult to guard against disaffirmation at a later date. In many cases, contracts with drunks are not enforceable.

Express and Implied Contracts:

In an *express contract,* whether written or oral, the terms of the contract or promises are clearly outlined. The contract states what each party will do. For example, "I agree to pay you $200 if you will repair my car."

---

* See Canadian Law, page 95.

An *implied contract* is one that is determined by the conduct of the parties. If you go to your dentist and have a tooth filled, you imply that you will pay for the work even though there was no express mention of the cost. However, if you asked the dentist ahead of time how much it would be and he quoted a dollar figure and you then agreed to the price and had the tooth filled, the contract would be express.

Today, merchandise and other goods carry an *implied warranty* that they are properly made and suited and safe for the uses or purposes for which they are sold. If there is a contractual warranty breach, you are entitled only to a money refund. However, under tort law, you have a right to collect for damages for personal injury. See the section on personal injuries for more information on implied warranties.

Interpretation of Contracts

The wording of contracts is not always clear-cut and precise. If the contract is not clear, arguments may arise and in some cases may result in litigation and a court case. The court will then have to interpret the contract based on what is stated and on rules that the courts have developed.

One of these rules is the *parol evidence rule*. Under contract law, the word "parol" means oral or written statements that have been made prior to the signing of the written contract. If a contract has been signed *that was intended to express the full terms of the contract,* the court will not permit evidence of discussions that occurred before the written contract was signed.

For example, suppose you are buying a house and the seller says, "I will leave the refrigerator, washing machine, and all the drapes." Yet, when you take possession, these items are gone. You have no recourse unless your signed purchase contract for the house (or a separate bill of sale) specifically lists these items as being included as part of the purchase.

There are some exceptions to the parol evidence rule which the court will consider if there is litigation:

1) If there is an indication or proof that the contract is the result of duress or fraud or is illegal;

2) If it can be shown that the written agreement does not include all the terms of the contract;

3) If the terms of the contract are vague or ambiguous.

Other rules of interpretation are the following:

1) Words will be given their plain and usual meaning, except when there is an accepted customary business usage or technical meaning within an industry;

2) Obvious mistakes in grammar or punctuation will be corrected by the court.

3) Ambiguous words will usually be ruled more unfavorably against the party that used them;

4) If there is conflict between a printed word and a written word, the written word will govern;

5) If there is a conflict between a figure numeral and a written numeral the written numeral will govern.

Time Element

Often, it is important that obligations or promises under the contract be performed exactly on time or performed before that time. For example, if a building is being constructed, it usually must be completed by a certain date. Often, there are penalty clauses requiring payment for each day or week beyond the specified time. If merchandise is ordered for sale on a certain date, it must be there by the date specified. If a person is moving out of a home and into another, the seller must be ready to give possession on the agreed upon date.

Contracts, then, often should specify the time by which the contract or parts of the contract are to be fulfilled. If there is no time provision, the courts will allow a reasonable time to act based on the circumstances. Where it is essential that the contract be fulfilled by a certain date, the contract should state "time is of the essence." This legal phrase indicates that a specific date is definitely intended, and, in such a case, the courts are unlikely to extend the deadline.

Breach of Contract

If one of the parties to a contract refuses to abide by its terms or performs only part of his obligation, he may be taken to court. A breach of contract may be complete or partial. Either way, the injured party is entitled to recover money damages for the value of the contract or the part that has not been fulfilled. For example, a construction company agrees to build a building for a certain amount of money by a certain date. By that date they have not started and now say they will not construct the building. They are in complete breach of the contract and may be sued for their nonperformance.

If a contract is only partially carried out or peformed defectively, there is a partial breach of contract. The injured party is entitled to a partial recovery depending on how much of the contract has not been completed.

Remedies for Broken Contracts

Awards are provided by the courts for breach of contract. The injured party is generally entitled to two different remedies: money damages or specific performance.

Money Damages:
The most common judicial method of dealing with proven

contractural breaches is the award of money damages. The amount awarded is compensation to the injured party for the losses he sustained because of the breach. The court attempts to measure the damages so as to put the injured party *in as good a position* as he would have been had the other party fulfilled his obligations under the contract. It is not intended that the injured party profit by the breach.

If your contract is broken by the other party, you may be awarded the profit you expected to make on the contract. If the contract would have caused you a loss, you have no case for damages.

The nonbreaching party usually has the duty to minimize his losses; that is, to mitigate the damages as much as possible. If someone agrees to buy machinery from you, and does not, you must make a reasonable attempt to sell to someone else. If you succeed, you must give the other party a credit for the amount you did receive. In other words, if the first party had agreed to pay $10,000, and you were able to sell the machinery for $8,000 to another party, the court could award you $2,000 in damages.

Specific Performance:*

Specific performance consists of a court order requiring a party who violated a contract to fulfill its terms. This is an extraordinary remedy and is applied only when an award of money would not compensate the injured party for his loss. It is normally used only when the subject matter of the contract is unique such as land, buildings, works of art, or antiques.

For example, if someone agrees to sell you a valuable original painting and then refuses to do so, you could sue for compliance on the basis that the item is unique. Money would not adequately compensate you. You cannot secure that painting elsewhere. The court could command the other party to comply with the contract.

---

* See Canadian Law, page 95.

If you wish to be assured that a sale will go through, write into the contract that the item is unique and that the contract may specifically be enforced. The contract could contain a clause stating that a business, land, or item is unique. For example, "The parties agree that the subject business, Hi-Tech Computer Co., is unique, and this contract for its purchase may be specifically enforced."

Defenses to Claims of Breach of Contract

There are a number of defenses to breach of contract. One, discussed earlier, is that the contract was not in writing in accordance with the Statute of Frauds. Other defenses are as follows:

Construing the Contract:

A principal defense of breach of contract is that there was no breach — that you have fulfilled your part of the contract. The terms of the contract are construed by you, (that is, interpreted) to show the suing party that you have fulfilled your obligations under the contract. This type of defense would most often be used if the contract is ambiguous or has omissions of some type. For example, if I contract with you to construct an addition to my home using Grade A materials, there could be an argument as to what Grade A means. Does it have a clear, definite meaning? Any contractual specifications must be clear.

Payment:

Payment in full is, of course, an obvious defense, but you must have proof. When making a final payment, get a signed receipt stating "paid in full," or endorse your check with some notation such as "Payment in full under contract of February, 16, 19—." Any cancelled check is a proof of full or partial payment.

227

Failure of Consideration:

Failure of consideration means that the suing party has not fulfilled his part of the contract; that is, that the goods or services for which the party is suing for payment were never delivered, or performed, or were not in accordance with the contract.

Release:

You can defend yourself against a breach of contract suit if you can show that you have a release from the other party stating that you have no further obligations under the contract. Releases should always be in writing and in many jurisdictions do not require consideration. Claimed oral releases are usually not upheld by the courts.

Equity:

There are a series of defenses known as "equity" or equitable defenses that may serve as justification for failure to fulfil a contract. Some of these reasons include fraud, duress, mutual mistake, impossibility, or unconsionability. The latter defense might be allowed if there was an obvious disadvantage in the bargaining power of the two parties and the contract itself was obviously unfair or "unconscionable." However, it could not be used just because you now wanted out of the contract or might lose money if you fulfilled the contract.

Statue of Limitations:

Time limits vary somewhat from state to state, but most states limit the time that suit may be brought to six years from the signing date of the contract.

Things to Remember

The general principles of contract law have been presented here. However, because of differences in state law and because of the complexities of many situations, you may need competent legal advise to protect your interests.

Preventative law is always the best law. *Always carefully read the terms of your contract* — including the small print. Read before you sign. If you do not understand a word or phrase or paragraph, ask for an explanation. If there is still a question in your mind, ask your lawyer.

Always obtain a copy of everything signed by you or others. Keep copies of all letters, checks, or receipts. Make notations of telephone calls or verbal statements that affect the contract. Never turn over an object of any value or document of significance without receiving a descriptive receipt or claim check. Protect your interests by utilizing the principles explained here.

Chapter 4
BUYING A HOME

The purchase of a home is the largest single financial transaction or investment that most of us will make in our lifetime. As a buyer, you need or want to purchase a home by a certain time and at the price you can afford to pay. You may find just the home you want in a short time but often your search may involve weeks.

Whatever the case, whenever you are buying a home you are entering into a legal contract and there are many legal problems involved or that may arise. Consequently, it is important that you know and understand the basic principles of real estate law in order to protect your investment.

How Much Can You Afford to Pay?

What you can afford to pay is not a legal question, but it is a determination you must make in advance to avoid possible legal or financial difficulties in the future.

As a general rule of thumb, you should not purchase a home for more or much more than three times your net annual pay. This means if your net "take-home pay" or other income is $50,000 you can afford a home costing $150,000. As a further rule, to be safe, monthly mortgage payments should not exceed one quarter of the family's monthly take-home pay or income.

The rules given are not necessarily easy to stay with and are often ignored. However, if you do go higher you may have to cut down on other items in your budget such as recreation, clothing, savings for your children's college education or your retirement, etc. Or, if you are fully confident of increased future income, you may have a tight squeeze on your budget until your income actually does go up.

Where Should You Start?

If you are moving into a new area or neighborhood, there

are several ways you may find out more about the area and the types of homes and residents it contains. You may have a friend who lives in or knows the area and can give you information. If you work for a large corporation, the corporation often has a real estate department which assists personnel who are being transferred or wish to purchase in a new area of the city. Newspaper real estate ads may be examined to get an idea of the area and the prices being asked.

Usually, however, the best method of finding the property you want is to consult a real estate broker. A broker's office is really a supermarket for homes. In the broker's office you read listings of homes, see photographs, determine to some degree that the homes you select for personal inspection seem to meet your requirements as to price and family needs.

Keep in mind, however, *the broker is the agent of the seller*. He works for the seller and will receive a commission only if he sells the property. The broker will assist you, guide you, advise you, but his interest is in selling the home to gain his commission. To a large degree, you must protect yourself and, in addition, once you have decided on a purchase, *you must employ a lawyer to protect your interests*.

Earnest Money Deposit

Once you decide you definitely wish to purchase a particular piece of property, it is usually wise to make a deposit and to secure a contract that prevents the seller from selling to someone else before the final contract of sale is drawn up and signed. The deposit you make is called the earnest money deposit. Often, the contract provides that the seller may retain the deposit if the proposed buyer does not sign a final contract for buying the property by a stipulated date.

The earnest money contract or receipt should contain the following elements:

1) It should identify by name both the seller and buyer.

2) It should clearly describe the property so that it can easily be identified.

3) It should stipulate the full purchase price of the property.

4) It should state what occurs to the deposit if the buyer defaults (does not actually purchase the property).

5) Since it is a legally enforceable contract, it should be signed by both parties.

The earnest money deposit will ultimately apply as part payment of the purchase price if the sale of the property is completed. The deposit may be an amount agreed upon such as $500 or a $1,000, or it may be a set percentage of the total selling price, such as 5 or 10 percent. The deposit agreement or receipt is not a substitute for the final sales agreement. It simply is a temporary contract stating the basic terms of the sale indicating that the final contract should be entered into on or before a certain date or the deposit will be forfeited.

Note: Many earnest money contracts protect the buyer by making the purchase contract contingent upon the availability of satisfactory financing. This is often the case when the buyer is attempting to secure a VA or FHA loan which is guaranteed by the federal government. In such a case, the contract becomes null and void if the buyer cannot obtain the financing. The buyer's deposit is then returned.

The Purchase and Sale Contract

All the precise details of the sale or purchase of a home must be contained in the purchase and sale contract. These elements include the full sales price, the legal description of the property, the type of title that will be conveyed, and so on. Areas of disagreement must be resolved while each side retains some bargaining power. Once the contract is signed, it is too late and both parties must abide by its terms.

Generally the seller's lawyer will prepare or draft the contract. It should then be submitted to the buyer's attorney for comment or change. If you are the buyer, your lawyer will advise you as to the meaning of any statements or provisions and will make any changes which he feels are essential or desirable in the contract.

From the buyer's point of view, the purchase contract must embody everything that he is purchasing. If an item is not specifically listed in the contract (or a separate bill of sale) there is no assurance that the buyer has a right to it at the time of settlement. This is particularly true of such items as kitchen appliances, carpeting, drapes, curtain rods, etc. Verbal statements have no validity once the contract is signed.

Purchase Contract Check List

Here is a check list of some of the important items that should be covered in your purchase contract.

Legal Description:

The most important single item in the contract is the legal description of the property. This description may simply be a verbatim statement taken from previous official records. However, if the land is part of a modern subdivision, the contract and the deed will merely state a lot and section number and then refer to a record book maintained in the county courthouse. It is advisable to include the street address as well as the legal description.

Prior to signing, the buyer should have a survey showing that the property conforms to local ordinances and that shows any restrictions, easements, or rights of way. Often the seller will have a previously completed survey that the buyer may use. The seller attaches a certificate that states that no changes (or what changes) have been made since the date of the survey.

If a new survey is to be made, the parties to the sale must agree on who pays for the survey.

Method of Payment:

Usually payment for the property is made in two parts. The first is the down payment, the amount of money to be paid upon signing the contract. If a preliminary earnest money deposit has been paid prior to the signing of the contract, this earnest money becomes part of the down payment. The second payment part is the amount that will be paid at the final closing.

The amount of the down payment is negotiable but usually is ten percent of the total price. How the down payment is to be handled should be specified in the contract. As the buyer, it is to your interest to try and ensure that the down payment is held in trust or escrow so that it can easily be recovered if the deal is not closed. However, if you are the seller, you may want no such restrictions placed on the down payment.

If the buyer must sell his present home in order to obtain the funds needed to buy the new home, or if his purchase is dependant on his ability to secure a mortgage, provisions stipulating that the sale is contingent on those events should be clearly stated in the contract. Unless the contract specifies that the buyer must sell his present house before he purchases the new home or that he must obtain a mortgage to finance the new home, and if either of these events do not occur before the closing date, the buyer may be in breach of contract or at the least, may lose his earnest money deposit.

It is, of course, to the seller's interest to oppose such provisions since an element of uncertainty enters into the contract. If he agrees to such a provision, the seller should require a time limitation so that if the buyer does not meet the requirement by a specified date, the contract becomes null and void and the seller may proceed to sell to someone else.

Inspection:

Although the buyer usually has visited the home one or more times, he oftentimes has not carefully inspected the house, and may not be qualified to do so. The contract should contain a provision permitting the buyer to have the house inspected by an engineer or other expert. If the inspection shows some structural or other fault (such as basement water leakage, termites, etc.), the buyer has the right to cancel the contract within a specified period of time and receive a refund of his down payment.

List Everything:

The contract should specifically state that the sale includes all the buildings, improvements, and all heating, plumbing, light fixtures, trees, shrubbery, etc., that are currently a part of the property. Also should be mentioned are built-in or permanent fixtures such as dish washers, refrigerators, kitchen ranges, or other items such as storm doors or windows, awnings, venetian blinds or shades, drapery rods, antennas, etc., unless it has been agreed they are to be removed. All too often, something such as a lighting fixture is not there when the new owner moves in.

Personal Property:

Items of personal property are not part of the real estate. However, if any such items are to be included as part of the purchase, they should be listed on a separate bill of sale. Personal property may include nonbuilt-in refrigerators, washing machines, carpeting, special chandeliers, drapes, work benches, etc. The items of personal property passing to the buyer should be separately listed and paid for as part of the total package at the closing.

Settlement Date:

The contract must specify a date on which the closing and

settlement will be made. The closing will usually be one to two months after the signing of the contract. This time period provides the time to make the title search, to have an inspection or survey made, and to secure financing. The closing may occur earlier than the original date set if both parties agree. If the contract is worded that "time is of the essence," the courts will usually require both parties to adhere strictly to the agreed upon date. Otherwise, if one of the parties is not prepared to close on the specified data, the courts will usually allow a reasonable extension of time without holding the party in breach of contract.

Possession:

The contract should specify the date on which the buyer may take possession or move in. Usually this is the day of closing. If, for example, the seller wishes to remain on the property after the closing, the contract should specify a date of possession and usually will provide for payment of rent for the period after the closing. Likewise, if the buyer wants possession earlier to paint or make repairs, etc. before the movers arrive, the contract should provide for rent to the seller for the period before the closing and a provision for ejecting the buyer if the latter does not proceed with the closing.

Form of Deed — Type of Title:*

Except by attorney's advise, the contract should provide that the seller will convey "fee simple title." This is the highest form of title. The title will be conveyed under a full covenant and *warranty deed* whereby the seller guarantees he is conveying good title to the property and free of any liens or encumbrances except those noted in the contract itself. There is another type of deed, called a *quit-claim deed* under which the seller guarantees nothing and which merely transfers whatever interest, if any, the seller may have in the property. Generally this type of deed is acceptable if the buyer's attorney

---

* See Canadian Law, page 96.

approves the deed and the buyer has obtained adequate title insurance.

Title Search — Title Insurance

Once the contract is signed, a title search will be made. (Surveys and inspections should also be made during the period preceding the closing.) There are "abstract companies" which search land records and report on problems or defects in the title. If a major defect is found, your attorney should advise you as to what action to take. If the title search or the survey reveals a minor defect (such as a neighbor's garage one or two inches over your property line), you as the buyer may refuse to close the deal. However, the seller may either agree to correct the problem or to reduce the purchase price to your benefit.

Title insurance is available in most states. For a relatively small amount, a title insurance company will guarantee a title against defects. Title insurance is well worthwhile and significantly increases the security of the property owner. Most lenders, such as banks, require that mortgage loans be covered by title insurance.

The Final Closing*
Settlement of the Sale

If all problems have been overcome, the closing or settlement will take place on the date specified in the contract. Often the closing takes place in the offices of the financial institution granting the mortgage or in their lawyer's office. Or it may be in the office of the title insurance company or the office of either the buyer's or seller's attorney. The deed and evidence of title are delivered to the buyer or his attorney for recording. The buyer must pay the balance of the purchase price usually by certified or cashier's check. The mortgage

---

* See Canadian Law, page 96.

secured by the buyer to obtain the purchase money is executed if not already signed. A bill of sale for the purchase of personal property and a copy of the survey should also be delivered to the buyer.

Prorations:

An important part of the closing will be the prorating of various charges against the property between the buyer and seller. These adjustments or prorations concern taxes, utilities, fuel, and water. In general, the seller pays for all taxes or services that cover his period of occupancy and will receive a credit for payments that he has made that will cover the buyer's occupancy.

Note: Before or by the closing, you must make sure that you are covered by homeowner's insurance. The financial institution issuing the mortgage will require evidence of this insurance, and you, of course, will want insurance for your own protection.

Chapter 5
RENTING

The large majority of us at sometime in our lives rent the place in which we live. Young married couples in particular who do not have the means to purchase a home immediately, rent until they do. The most common form of rented dwelling, particularly in cities, is an apartment. But there are two-family dwellings where the owner lives on one floor and rents the other. Or single-family homes or condominiums may be rented out by their owner. Knowing what to look for in leases and knowing what your rights are as a tenant, can save you money and unnecessary aggravation or frustration.

The Lease

The lease is a *contract* entered into between the landlord and a tenant. The lease describes the place being rented and sets forth the landlord's and tenant's mutual rights and obligations.

A lease can be oral, but almost always it is a written (or preprinted) document that gives the tenant the right of possession for a specific length of time. The lease is a legally enforceable contract and should set forth all the terms and conditions that bind both the landlord and tenant for the term of the lease.

Read and Understand Your Lease

All leases must, of course, have a description of the apartment or property being rented. Aside from this description, following are the most common provisions or elements of a lease. Most of the provisions apply equally to either commercial or residential leases.

FAMILY LEGAL GUIDE

Lease Provisions

Rental Payments:

Rent is the amount paid for the right to occupy the space described in the lease. Almost always, rent is paid in advance. Most residential leases run for one to three years, and the amount of rent is usually determined on a yearly basis but payable monthly. Although you pay monthly, you are legally obligated for the rent for the entire term of the lease, once you have signed it.

Rent is usually a flat amount for the period involved. But there are leases that provide for gradually increased payments at specified intervals to compensate the landlord for increased expenses or for other reasons. Or the lease may specify that, if such things as taxes, utilities, etc. increase, the landlord may collect "additional rental." Be sure you know the rental provisions of your lease.

In any event, the lease should state the amount of the monthly rental installments, where it is to be paid (at the landlord's office, to his agent, etc.), and the specific date by which payment is due. If payment is not made within a certain time limit, the landlord has the right to evict the tenant and/or sue for back rent. It is also common for landlords to charge a late fee for delinquent rental payments.

Security Deposit:

To protect themselves, most landlords require what is called a "security deposit." This deposit is protection against the tenant's abandoning the property, nonpayment of rent, damage to the property, or failing to properly maintain it.

Security deposits are payable in advance and usually are the equivalent of one or two month's rent. If the tenant is not in default of the lease, and has not damaged the property, the deposit is sometimes applied against the last month or months of the lease. Upon expiration of the lease, the security deposit is to be returned in full, unless the landlord has a valid claim against the tenant. If the tenant leaves the apartment in filthy condition or in need of repair, the landlord may be entitled to deduct from the deposit an amount to cover the cost of cleaning or repair.

Some states require that the landlord pay interest on the security deposit. You should determine the law in your state and what the rate of interest is, if any. In some states, the landlord is required to refund the deposit within a stipulated period (perhaps 30 to 45 days) after the tenant moves. If he does not, or if he fails to pay required interest or makes unwarranted damage claims, the tenant may sue. Suit may be brought in Small Claims Court where no attorney is required. However, some states require a defaulting landlord to pay attorney's costs as well as court costs so the tenant may wish to sue in a regular court.

If the lease does not provide that the deposit be applied against the last month's rent, many tenants (if they are planning to move out) fail to pay the last months' rent and thereby use up the deposit. There is no legal basis for doing so, but, because of the short period involved, the landlord can do little. There may be arguments concerning damages or improper maintenance, but hopefully both parties will be fair.

Options to Renew or Purchase:

An *option* is a right or privilege of doing something. An *option to renew* gives you, the tenant, the right to renew your lease at the end of your present lease, even if at a higher rent. Although some landlords resist such options, try to secure an option to renew your apartment or other lease, without added cost whenever possible.

An *option to purchase* will usually not be found in apartment leases unless the apartment building is being converted to co-ops or condominiums. But they do appear or apply where you are renting a duplex, a condominium, or a home. An option to purchase is always good to get. It not only protects your occupancy but also enables you to profit from an increase in the value of the property. Such options are common in leases of commercial or industrial structures. In some cases the rent may be applied as part of the final purchase price.

Subleases and Assignments:

Unless a lease provides to the contrary, a tenant may assign or sublet his apartment. A *sublease* is allowing someone to use only part of the premises or all of them for a period shorter than the full term of the lease. An *assignment* is a transfer to another person of the entire interest of the tenant in the lease for the remaining term of the lease.

Many residence leases restrict or prohibit the right of a tenant to sublease or assign. Most apartment leases provide that the apartment cannot be assigned or sublet without the landlord's prior written consent. Some states have laws that provide that a landlord must be reasonable in giving his consent, and many leases so provide.

In any event, secure the landlord's permission before allowing someone else to take possession of your rented home or apartment. Where the lease contains a clause against subleasing, the tenant must pay the rent for the full term whether he continues to occupy the premises or not.

Alterations:

In commercial leases, there is often a provision that the landlord will make certain alterations before the tenant moves in. These alterations should, of course, clearly be spelled out. The tenant is not obligated under the terms of the lease unless the alterations are made.

If the tenant, of either commercial or residential property, wishes to make alterations either before or after moving in, he usually must have prior permission of the landlord. If the alteration includes fixtures, the fixtures will normally belong to the landlord at the termination of the lease unless the tenant and landlord have agreed otherwise in writing. Some leases provide that alterations must be removed and the apartment or building be returned to its original condition at the tenant's expense upon termination.

Repairs:

Most leases provide that upon termination of the lease, the property must be returned to the landlord in the condition it was originally leased except for normal wear and tear. Probably no other provision of a lease causes more problems than the one that requires the tenant to maintain the premises and keep it in good repair.

Normally, the lease provides that the landlord is responsible for structural repairs, such as the roofs and outside walls, and for outside maintenance such as parking lots and walkways. However, some lease forms provide that the tenant is responsible for interior repairs such as to the plumbing, stoves or refrigerators, leaky faucets, etc. Further, the lease may stipulate that the tenant is responsible for damage that results from such causes as water leakage of plumbing, short circuits, steam, gas, etc.

From the tenants viewpoint, the best clause to have in a lease is one that says he is responsible only for interior repairs of a minor nature, or only such repairs as result from his own misuse or fault. All other repairs will then be the responsibility of the landlord.

Check your lease carefully to see what services you can expect without cost and what services or damages you are responsible for. In the event of a mishap, you may be liable for a substantial cost. An apartment dweller's insurance policy is a good idea to protect yourself from damage loss both to the apartment and to your furniture and other personal belongings.

Other Provisions:

Other common provisions of rental leases include the following:

1) Pets (often they are prohibited)

2) Garbage or rubbish disposal

3) Use of laundry facilities and storage areas

4) Periodic painting

5) Extermination of rats or bugs

6) Heat, running water, and hot water

7) Landlord's right of entry to the premises (under what conditions)

8) Noise or other disturbances

9) Responsibility for snow or ice removal

10) Parking or garage facilities (additional rent?)

Getting Along With Your Landlord*

Hopefully, if you rent you will have a satisfactory and friendly relationship with your landlord. But friendly relations disappear quickly if either party fails to meet their obligations under the lease.

The most frequent problems are caused by failure of the landlord to provide proper service and by nonpayment of rent by the tenant. Tenants sometimes withhold rent if the landlord has failed to make certain repairs or has provided inadequate heat. Before withholding rent make sure you have given the landlord written notice of the problems you say exist. You may deliver the notice personally, but a better method is by certified mail, return receipt requested. Keep a copy of the

* See Canadian Law, *Residential Tenancy Legislation*, page 96.

notice and the return receipt so that you will have them readily available.

Many municipalities, particularly large cities, have housing offices, departments, or bureaus that investigate tenant's complaints. These agencies are empowered to enforce housing regulations or lease provisions if the landlord fails to remedy violations. The most important obligation with which a landlord must comply is called a "warranty of habitability." This warranty guarantees the tenant that during the period of the lease no condition will exist in the building or the apartment which would render it unfit for human habitation or that is detrimental to life, health, or safety. Some states have ruled that this warranty is implied whether or not stated in the lease. Some courts have interpreted the warranty broadly to include falling plaster or cracked walls, peeling paint, and leaky plumbing.

Many leases provide that rent may not be withheld because of poor service. If you withhold rent, the landlord may bring eviction proceedings against you. You may then be faced with legal expense and the possibility of being evicted from your apartment. Try to get a local government housing or health agency to help you. If you cannot secure help, your only alternative to withholding rent is to sue the landlord or to get other tenants to join with you in some concerted action.

Tenant Defaults — Evictions*

If you fail to pay rent without legal justification, you are in default. The landlord may then proceed with eviction proceedings. Some states require that the landlord notify the tenant of any violation before filing for eviction or terminating the lease. The tenant has the opportunity to pay the rent or to correct any other alleged violation of the lease within a specified period.

A majority of states have a procedure whereby landlords

---

* See Canadian Law, *Termination of Tenancies*, page 97.

can quickly take tenants to court, both to evict them and to secure payment of past due rent. The tenant may first learn of this action when court papers are served on him. The papers give a date and time by which the tenant must appear to answer the charges against him. In the court, the tenant will be given the chance to explain why he has not paid the rent. If he has a legal justification, the court will consider it. On the other hand, if he now wants to remain and pays the rent then and there, the court will usually allow the payment and dismiss the eviction.

Ejection:

In some jurisdictions there is a legal action called *ejectment* or some similar term. Ejectment is not brought to secure payment of past due rent. Instead, it is for the purpose of ejecting a tenant who has defaulted on some *substantial obligation* of the lease. A principal such obligation recognized in all states is failure to vacate the property rented upon expiration of the lease. Other reasons might be:

1) Making alterations to the property without approval.

2) Subletting the apartment without approval.

3) Keeping pets without approval.

4) Damaging the apartment or other parts of a building.

5) Behaving offensively, such as failure to remove garbage or dumping it in unauthorized places.

6) Noisy or other behavior that disturbs other tenants.

If failure to vacate is the problem, you can be evicted even if you offer the rent. If the landlord accepts the rent you become a month-to-month tenant and the landlord can evict or cancel you on one month's notice.

Tenant Holdovers

If you retain possession after expiration of a lease, you are termed a *holdover*. Depending on the law in your state or on specific provisions in your original lease, your lease may or may not be renewed for another full term the same length as your original lease. Unless provided otherwise, in some states the holdover status only means that the lease is renewed for another month. (The landlord may choose to eject you, unless the lease provides for a renewal.)

Most leases do provide for holdovers. Usually the lease states that if the tenant occupies the premises at the end of the term, the lease will automatically be renewed or in force for a month, or a year, or whatever other period is specified in the lease. Often, the tenant must notify the landlord thirty days or more in advance of his intent to either remain or vacate.

Landlord Defaults

Landlords, too, may violate the lease agreement. The landlord may fail to make repairs or fail to provide needed services such as heat and hot water, and as a result the premises are inhabitable. In such a case, the tenant can claim that he has unlawfully been evicted because of the landlord's failure. If the tenant can legally substantiate his claim, he is not obligated to pay rent until the default is corrected. However, as mentioned earlier in the section on "Getting Along With Your Landlord," there are dangers to the withholding of rent unless there is legal authorization or justification.

In some jurisdictions, if you can prove that a landlord has failed to furnish agreed upon services or has failed to make repairs, the court may award you a rent reduction to cover the loss of the services or benefit of the repairs. In other cases, the tenant may also have a claim for damages if there is damage to his personal property, if he has to leave the premises temporarily, or if he has to find other housing because of the landlord's violation of the lease.

Violations of leases occur on both sides. If the landlord fails to observe his substantial obligations under the lease, the tenant generally has the right to vacate the property or apartment and be released from the lease without any further liability. As mentioned, in some cases, the tenant may even be able to collect damages.

Chapter 6
YOU, THE LAW, AND YOUR JOB

In the historical past, employees had few legal rights. However, today there are federal and state laws that do much to protect a worker's employment rights and working conditions. Organized labor, too, provides protection through collective bargaining. In addition, there are various public and private agencies that aid the employee in dealing with unemployment or work related problems. Here we will review some of the important laws that protect or set forth your rights as well as the rights of unions or employers.

Employer and Employee Rights
Protective Legislation*

The National Labor Relations Act of 1935

The NLRA was enacted to permit and regulate union activity and to prevent employer domination of the unions. The Act gave unions the right to bargain collectively with employers for the benefit of employees in such areas as pay, job tenure, and working conditions. The Act is administered by the National Labor Relations Board (NLRB), and the Board is responsible for hearing grievances under the Act and other federal labor legislation. States have their own agencies to deal with labor matters concerning employers within the state who are not engaged in interstate commerce.

The Taft-Hartley Act of 1947

This Act essentially covers the same areas as the NLRA but goes further prohibiting the following:

1) Forbids forcing workers to join a union before being hired (called a "closed shop"). Although closed shops are prohibited, "union shops" are permitted whereby a nonunion member can be hired, but unless he (or she) joins the union within a specified time, he may lose his job.

---

* For Canadian employment and human rights legislation, see page 98.

2) Forbids such labor practices as secondary boycotts, feath-
erbedding, or jurisdictional strikes.

3) Forbids the forcing of employers to discriminate against
an employee.

4) Forbids the imposition by unions of excessive or discriminatory fees or dues in a union shop.

5) Forbids a union to refuse to bargain collectively with an
employer.

The T-H Law, then, permits "union shops" whereby nonunion workers can be hired, but once hired, they must join a
union by a specified period of time (usually 60 to 120 days).
If the worker does not join, the employer must discharge him.
It protects the rights of individual employees not to strike and
provides for grievance presentation without union representation. In addition, it provides for a "cooling-off" period
whereby strikes are prevented for eighty days in interstate
commerce which, if permitted to occur, would imperil the
national safety or health.

Certain states have passed "right-to-work" laws whereby
every worker has the right to work whether he wants to join
the union or not. Such a law makes it illegal to fire employees
who are not union members even if there is a union contract
with a union shop provision.

Fair Labor Standards Act

First enacted in 1938, the Act has since been amended and
undoubtedly will be amended in the future as conditions change.
The Act provides for certain minimum wages and maximum
working hours. The majority of states have similar laws to
cover workers who are not covered by the federal law. However, state laws vary considerably concerning minimum wages,
overtime pay, hours, and age. If you are concerned, check the
law of your state.

Under the Act the kind of work children can do is limited. For example, young people under 16 cannot be employed on construction jobs, use power-driven machines, work as public messengers, or work in certain industries such as manufacturing, mining, transportation, or in public utilities. *Persons not covered by the Act* include executives, administrative personnel, certain transportation employees, seasonal industry employees, outside salesmen, and handicapped workers and students with government approval.

The Act provides that an employer may not fire an employee who files a complaint or suit. Where a violation occurs, the employee may sue for double the wages due him, plus attorneys' fees and court costs provided he does so within two years of the violation. Enforcement of the Act is under the jurisdiction of the Wage and Hour Division of the U.S. Department of Labor.

Equal Employment Opportunity Commission

The Equal Employment Opportunity Commission (EEOC) was set up by the Civil Rights Act of 1964. The Act prohibits employers, unions, and employment agencies from discriminating in employment or membership on the basis of race, religion, national origin, or sex. In addition to the EEOC, most states have their own civil-rights or equal-rights commissions.

As indicated, the purpose of the Act is to protect workers against discriminatory practices in hiring, firing, promotion, or job tenure. Other federal or state laws prohibit discrimination because of age or physical handicap. Exceptions to these laws are where age is an important criterion, where certain physical abilities are needed, or where heavy physical work is required.

Sexual Harassment

Under the Civil Rights Act of 1964, sexual harassment is

one of the prohibited practices. Although difficult to fully define, sexual harassment may include the following:

1) Unwelcome advances of a sexual nature.

2) Oral or physical conduct of a sexual nature.

3) Expressing or implying that sexual submission is a requirement for continued employment.

4) When sexual conduct interferes with work performance or creates a hostile, offensive, or intimidating work environment.

Sexual harassment can be difficult to prove and innocent parties can be damaged. Employers should carefully investigate any cases brought to their attention and take immediate action to avoid a formal complaint or proceedings.

If you feel you are being harassed make your feelings clearly known to the offending party. If that fails, speak to the person's superior (if there is one). If that fails, file a complaint at your local EEOC office.

Occupational Safety and Health Act

Enacted in 1970 and since amended, the federal Occupational Safety and Health Act (OSHA) establishes health and safety standards that employers must follow for the well-being and protection of their employees. All states have similar laws.

Specifically designed to eliminate or minimize work hazards, the Act covers buildings, furnishings, equipment and machinery, construction, and fire or other work hazards. Generally, where there are building code, or fire regulation, or similar violations, complaint to a state or city agency should be sufficient. However, where there are serious violations such as chemical pollution, explosive hazards, or irradiation, complaint to the federal Department of Labor may be better.

Workers' Compensation

All states have workmens' compensation laws. These laws were passed to provide for industrial safety and financial compensation where injuries are work related. Although the state laws vary somewhat, they all include the following:

1) Where there is a work-related injury or death, the employee is compensated by a predetermined schedule of benefits no matter what caused the accident or who might be at fault.

2) Injuries for which the employee may be compensated include total or partial loss of use of various body parts, temporary or permanent disability, permanent injuries, disfigurement, and occupational diseases.

3) Necessary medical care must be provided in addition to any cash compensation that may be awarded.

4) In the event of death, benefits are payable to dependents.

5) Benefits are based on a percentage of the person's weekly or monthly wage, and are payable for a set number of weeks up to a maximum total amount. Two-thirds of a person's average earnings usually is the upper limit for income benefits.

Medical payments are in addition to income payments and make some provision for surgery, prosthetic devices to restore limb or other functions, as well as for rehabilitation training. If the employer does not provide medical care (through a health/hospitalization plan or otherwise), the employee may secure medical care on his own and submit his expenses when he files for compensation.

When an injury or illness occurs, the employee should file a claim with the proper state agency. Generally, the employer will assist with the filing of the claim. However, whatever the situation, the employer must immediately be notified of the claim. Failure to notify the employer may result in the claim being denied. The state agency will determine whether compensation will be allowed, and if so, in what amount and for what period.

Unemployment Compensation

If a person involuntarily loses his job, he (or she) is eligible for unemployment insurance or compensation. To be eligible a person must have been previously employed in work covered by the plan, have the ability to work, be available for work, and actively looking for work.

If you lose your job involuntarily, and are covered by unemployment insurance, apply immediately to the nearest state unemployment office. Bring your Social Security Card, your discharge notice, and your pay records for the last five calendar quarters. Your earnings in your highest-paying quarter will determine the amount of your benefit. Since the benefits vary from state to state, you will have to find out from your state office the amount to which you are entitled.

The main purposes of unemployment insurance are to:

1) Provide income during periods of involuntary unemployment;

2) Give a person time to secure or regain employment.

3) Aid a person in securing employment for which qualified.

State employment services provide assistance in securing a new job or position through counseling, job listings, and training programs. Refusal to accept a suitable position may result in loss of benefits. Benefit loss may also occur if the worker is receiving workman's compensation, a pension, or severance pay.

Social Security*

What might be termed "regular" Social Security provides retirement benefits at age 62 or 65. However, at any age, a person may be eligible for disability payments. To be eligibile, a person must be unable to earn a living and the disability condition must have lasted or be expected to last for at least a year. The disability may be either mental or physical. Persons who may have a disability should contact their nearest Social Security office for application information.

Veteran's Rights

If you are a veteran, you are entitled to certain rights under the G.I. Bill of Rights. For detailed information, contact your nearest Veterans Administration office. Some of the principal rights available to you if you qualify include:

1) Home loan guarantee.

2) Medical care or treatment for service-connected disabilities.

3) Pensions or compensation for disabled veterans for service-connected disabilities.

4) Educational assistance.

5) Right to reclaim a former job or position.

Other Protection

Aside from the protection employees are provided under the federal or state laws discussed earlier, there are some protections available that do not fall under a specific law.

Union Protection:
Individuals who are members of a union that has a contract

---

* See Canadian Law, page 99.

with the employer are protected by whatever provisions are contained in the collective bargaining agreement. If you are fired or feel that there are violations of your rights under union-negotiated agreements, you should immediately report your firing or the suspected violations to your union officials. Many collective-bargaining agreements stipulate that employees may not be discharged without good cause and these will be enforced by a court.

If you feel there has been a violation of your civil or human rights, talk to your union representative first, if you are a union member. If you do not belong to a union or get no satisfaction from your union, go to a regional office of the EEOC. They will assist you in the preparation of a formal complaint. If it is appropriate to do so, they will refer you to a state agency.

Both the EEOC and state agencies tend to be proemployee and prominority where business or industry are concerned. In many cases these agencies may bring about reinstatement of jobs, back pay, damages, or fines of the employer.

Grievance Against a Union:

A person having a grievance against the union should first make use of the union's grievance machinery. His local shop steward can help him with the proper procedure. The union must make available to him a copy of the collective bargaining agreement with the company. If they do not do so, the complainant can complain directly to the federal Department of Labor. If the union gives no satisfaction and he has a legitimate complaint, the worker can sue the union or its officials, and he is protected from union retaliation.

Nonunion Employees

Persons who do not belong to unions and are thus not protected by collective bargaining, or who do not have an individual employment contract, or who cannot show discrimination in some way, can be fired *at will* by their employers.

Legally, "at will" means that the employment can be terminated either by the employer or the employee at any time, without reason or prior notice. The employee can quit at any time if he wishes, but also, the employer can fire him at any time, with or without reason. These rules have been long-established under common law.

In some states, and in certain types of cases, there has been some limitation concerning the discharge of employees "at will." Many of these cases come under a fairly new legal doctrine which is called "abusive discharge." In some cases, the court has found there was an implied contract that prevented the employee from being fired except for good cause.

The discharge of persons who stand up for their rights or call attention to law violations may be held to be abusive. This includes persons who have been fired because they complained of unsafe working conditions, sexual harrassment, falsifying of financial or other records, price fixing, etc.

The firing of workers who filed for workmen's compensation has been held to be abusive. Employees who have been fired shortly before becoming eligible for pension rights or severance pay rights have had their employment and rights restored. In a few cases, courts have held that the employer had a tort liability; that is, by his acts he wrongfully injured the employee, and the employee has the right to recover damages. However, statistically, there are few cases where the discharge of an "at will" employee will not be upheld by the courts.

Chapter 7
LAW AND THE FAMILY*

Marriage is a civil contract but it has one aspect that makes it different from other contracts. It cannot be terminated at will by the two persons involved. It is binding until death of one of the parties, unless the marriage is dissolved by the state; that is, by a divorce or annulment.

Valid and Invalid Marriages

The validity of a marriage is determined by the laws of the state in which it takes place. A marriage that is legal where it took place is legal anywhere in the United States.

In most states, for a marriage to be valid, the following formalities are required:

1) Both persons must have reached a legal age specified by the state to marry without the consent of their parents. The age varies somewhat from state to state but most commonly is 18.

2) A marriage license must be issued. The license is legal permission to marry and is issued by a local marriage license bureau, court, or other authorized agency.

3) In most states, both applicants are required to undergo laboratory blood tests to show that they are free of veneral disease.

4) A marriage ceremony must be performed within a specified period by a clergyman, judge, or other court appointed person.

Persons who have not reached the legal age specified by the state can marry in most states if they have the consent of their parents. If a minor lies about his (or her) age and is married, the marriage is invalid and the parent or guardian

---

* For Canadian family and married persons rights, see page 99.

can have the marriage annulled; that is, declared legally invalid.

Common-Law Marriages

In a common-law marriage, the two partners live together as man and wife and either agree to be married or consider themselves married even though they have not secured a license or gone through the marriage ceremony. Common-law marriages are legal in some states but not valid in others. If a common-law marriage is contracted legally in one state, it will usually be considered valid in other states.

Living Together

Many states have laws making *cohabitation* (living together without benefit of marriage) illegal. However, these laws are rarely enforced, and socially such arrangements have become more acceptable.

Couples who live together, may have agreements, either written or oral, concerning expenses, household duties, property rights, and other. If they live together, one party may be able to collect money or other property from the other party if their relationship is dissolved, but only if there is an express or implied contract. One must have promised something and the other must prove it. To do so, it is best, of course, to have all agreements or promises in writing. Even better in many cases, is the actual transfer of assets from one party to the other, either outright transfer or in trust. In some states, since no valid marriage has taken place, the court may rule that any agreements are unenforceable since the relationship is illegal.

Termination of Marriage

Because marriage is a contract protected by state laws, it can only be dissolved before the death of one of the parties by a judicial act. Basically, there are three legal methods by which a marriage may be dissolved or suspended — divorce, separation, and annulment. A marriage may also be terminated by the unexplained absence of a spouse for a fixed number of years. The spouse is then presumed dead.

Divorce:

Divorce is a dissolution of a marriage — a complete break up of a validly contracted arrangement. Since marriage is governed by state law, the rules for procedure and the grounds for filing for divorce must be based on the laws of the state where the spouse bringing the action resides.

No-fault Divorce:

The majority of states have some form of *no-fault divorce*. No-fault divorce differs from conventional divorce in that no evidence of misconduct and fault on the part of either spouse is required for filing. Usually, the only ground needed is "irreconcilable differences," "incompatibility," or "irretrivable breakdown." Some states require that an attempt be made, through counseling, to reconcile the differences of the couple. If the attempt fails, either party can file for divorce.

If the couple has lived apart for a year or two under a court approved separation decree or a valid written separation agreement, this fact may be sufficient grounds for divorce in some states.

Divorce by Fault

Following are the grounds for termination of the marriage usually provided for in those states that still require proof of "fault."

1) Adultery

2) Refusal or inability to cohabit

3) Desertion or abandonment

4) Non-support

5) Cruel treatment — either physical or mental

6) Conviction of a crime and/or imprisonment for a stated period

7) Insanity

8) Habitual drunkenness

Residence Requirement

Most states require that a person who wants to bring a divorce action must reside in the state for a certain period of time before bringing suit. Typically, waiting periods are three months, or a year. Nevada has a six-week waiting period.

Separation:

Separation is a status in which the marriage continues but the husband and wife agree to live separately and provisions are made for support, child custody, and property disposition.

When a separation is sought by court decree, all the legal steps and grounds that are involved in a divorce decree are required. If the parties agree voluntarily to separation by written agreement no grounds need be given. There also may be separation by tacit agreement. The two parties simply live apart and have an informal understanding of their relationship.

While separated, the couples cannot remarry. Unless stated otherwise in the agreement, all rights of inheritance and duty to support would continue. Informal separation offers the best hope of later reconciliation. In most cases, formal separation later leads to divorce.

Annulment:

A divorce dissolves a valid marriage. An annulment makes

a marriage void as if it had never taken place or existed. In some states, annulment action must be brought within a certain period of time. Annulment actions, in general, must follow the same procedures as for divorce except there may be a greater burden of proof with corroborating evidence needed.

Annulment is by court decree. Grounds for annulment may be as follows depending on the state law:

1) Marriage to a minor or by minors

2) Fraud in inducing the marriage (including homosexuality and unwillingness to have children)

3) Failure or inability to consumate the marriage

4) Bigamy

5) An incestuous marriage

6) Marriage in another state to avoid local provisions

7) Force or threat in inducing the marriage

8) Insanity or idiocy

The number of annulments has declined substantially in states that provide for no-fault divorce.

Custody of Children

Whether parents seek divorce or annulment or simply separate, provision must be made for the support and custody of the children. The sole consideration should be the welfare of the child. However, oftentimes this is not true. The child becomes a pawn in the divorce or separation proceedings. There is no one (except perhaps the court) to represent his interests.

The divorce degree or separation agreement will settle the question of custody. However, because of changed circumstances, the court may change the custodial provisions at any time. If a parent could not provide a proper home at the time of the original proceeding but can now do so, the court may award custody provided there is supporting reason to do so.

In the past, the courts usually favored the mother for custody where the child was 12 years or younger, unless the father could prove the mother "unfit." This is still largely true. However, there is some willingness of more and more judges to grant custody to the father. Courts have held that the father has as much right as the mother to custody of a child under 12 provided the father strongly wants custody, has good economic prospects, and has the time and willingness to subordinate his interests and activities to those of the child. However, there is still a strong preference of judges to award young children to the mother.

If a child is more than twelve, judges will generally consult a child as to which parent the child prefers. If the child seems to have a good understanding of the situation and expresses a strong choice, the judge will usually award custody to the preferred parent provided the parent is able and willing.

Visitation rights are usually equally important with the custodial rights. Such rights are subject to negotiation and agreement. Usually, if the parents agree on a visitation schedule, the judge will agree. However, the trial judge may use his own discretion.

Alimony and Child Support

There are two types of payment that are a basic part of matrimonial cases — alimony and child support. The payments may be either by court decree or payments required under a separation agreement. Alimony, also, may be of two types:

Temporary Alimony:
While an action for divorce or separation is pending, tem-

porary alimony may be awarded by the court. The award is made so that a spouse (usually the wife) will have support while the action is proceeding and before a final decree is entered. The temporary alimony is usually determined by the judge on the basis of financial statements and tax returns of the parties. Often, if the wife is the one suing, the husband will be required to pay the wife's legal fees in addition to the alimony.

Permanent Alimony:

Permanent alimony is fixed by the final court decree. In determining the amount, the court considers the current and future financial status of the parties, years of marriage, age and number of children, social standing, and which party was at fault, if any. The decree will stipulate whether the alimony will continue for a certain number of years, until the remarriage of the spouse receiving alimony, or until the death of either spouse.

Men may receive alimony, but such awards are rare. A wealthy wife could be required to support her husband if there is great disparity in their individual wealth or if he is disabled by age or physically infirm. A decree of alimony may be modified by the court if it can be shown that there are substantially changed financial conditions or perhaps concealed assets at the time of the original decree or agreement.

In most large urban areas, the combined alimony and child support payments or award often is about one-third of the husband's income before taxes. However, it could vary from twenty to forty percent depending on total circumstances.

Child Support:

Payments for child support are usually stated separately from alimony. However, they are often considered within the percentage being allowed the receiving spouse. Child support is usually stated in specific weekly or monthly support amounts and normally will continue until the child is of age or until schooling is completed. Unless the law is changed, child-support payments are treated differently than alimony for tax purposes and therefore should be stated separately.

Lump-Sum Settlements:

At times, a wife may want her alimony paid in one lump sum rather than in periodic installments. In addition to a sum of money, such lump-sum settlements may provide for real estate to be transferred from one spouse to the other, or for release of one spouse's interest in real estate to the other. The agreement may also provide for the distribution of personal property such as cash, stocks and bonds, automobiles, furniture, and other property.

Voluntary Agreements

A judge can change the alimony set by a court decree, but he cannot change alimony or other provisions that have been made by an enforceable surviving marital agreement. It is, therefore, good to seek a favorable separation agreement that will survive or go beyond any court decree.

Marital agreements may not only cover alimony and child support but also may provide for life insurance or health insurance payments. Since alimony ceases on the death of a husband, life insurance provides the wife with future protection. A marital agreement may also peg future alimony payments to the husband's income. If his income goes up/the alimony goes up. Other provisions may cover possession and maintenance of the family home and inheritance rights of either children or a spouse on the death of the other.

Property Distribution

Historically, alimony alone often has not been satisfactory for women. As part of a divorce agreement, many husbands settle capital or property on their wives. They may do so partly out of a sense of fairness and partly to induce the wife to agree to a divorce. Often the family home is given to the wife even though it was entirely in the husband's name and the wife could not have received full title from the court.

In states that have "dower," "curtesy," or community property laws, each spouse has certain rights in the marital property. In states which do not provide for these rights, each spouse usually keeps what is in his or her own name upon marital separation.

In New York, because of inequities that may exist, the judge has been empowered to make an "equitable distribution" of the family assets. No special rule or pattern of distribution has yet been established, but, in general, the longer the time duration of the marriage the greater the rights. Equitable distribution may also occur because of separate marital agreements, or by *premarital* agreements whereby the distribution of certain rights to property has been agreed upon in advance of the marriage.

Enforcement of Alimony Payments or Agreements

Not all states recognize permanent alimony. It is therefore important to know the laws of your state before taking any action. It is always good to have a separation agreement which can be consolidated into the divorce decree. Such consolidation permits the court to enforce the decree or agreement by contempt proceedings. A separation agreement is a contract. Like any other contract, it can be the basis of a suit if one of the parties breaches it.

Get a Good Lawyer

In the event of a matrimonial dispute and likely separation or divorce, it is most important to engage a strong lawyer early. Look for a tough, experienced marital case lawyer who will fight if necessary.

Family friends are often not good lawyers to engage. The bonds of friendship may interfere. However, in some cases, the mutual friendship may bring a reconciliation or a less acrimonious settlement. Settling the dispute out of court is by far the best solution to seek.

Matrimonial settlements should be based on hardheaded, non-sentimental judgments. Don't give too much or accept too little. The agreement may be for a long time, and times and conditions change. Allowance for change should be made.

Chapter 8
WILLS AND ESTATES

Unfortunately, everyone dies. A properly drawn will is the means whereby you can dispose of your property — your estate — the way you want and to whom you want. Having no will, or an improperly drawn or executed will, may cause disaster for loved ones. It can cause unnecessary litigation, unnecessary taxes, undesired results, and other problems.

For purposes of planning your will, your estate is everything you own of monetary value. It includes your home or other real estate. It includes your bank and savings accounts, stocks and bonds, life insurance, rights under a pension plan, art objects, stamp or coin collections, automobiles, furniture, or any other personal item you may own. A will ensures that your loved ones will receive the property you want them to have at a minimum of taxes and expense.

What is a Will?

A will is a signed written document in which the person making the will specifies how and to whom his (or her) property will go after death. The male maker of a will is known as a *testator* and a female as a *testatrix*.

Types of Wills*

A will may be written by the testator in his or her own handwriting. This is called a *holographic will*. The will may or may not be witnessed. In some states, the will may be admitted into probate under certain circumstances of proof even though there may be no witnesses. However, a holographic will may well be ruled invalid. It should only be used in a real emergency or unusual circumstances.

Ordinarily, a will is prepared by a lawyer, typed in his office, and then signed by you there in front of witnesses. There should be at least two witnesses and some states require

* See Canadian Law, page 101.

three. You must state the document you are signing is your will, and the witnesses attest by signing below your name, that you did sign the will on a specific date.

The witnessing requirement is an essential requirement of a validly executed will. Upon your death, the witnesses may be called upon to testify that you signed the will in their presence. The witness does not read the will. He merely attests to your statement that it is your will and attests to your signature. The lawyer often acts as one of the witnesses.

It is important that you carefully read and understand your will. Are the persons or groups getting what you wanted them to have? The lawyer may have misunderstood you, or you may feel something could be confused, or you may even have changed your mind. If so, the will will have to be reworded and retyped. Hand changes are not valid. Read the will carefully and slowly. Is it exactly what you want? Never sign the will unless you understand and agree with every word.

Information the Lawyer Needs

To properly draft a will the lawyer needs certain information. The information that is vital to the proper preparation of the will is as follows:

1) Names, ages, and addresses of the testator, his spouse, children, and others who might be or are beneficiaries under the will.

2) A list of all assets of the testator and spouse. These should include:
   a) The home and any other real property and its value.
   b) Stocks, bonds, investments including IRA's.
   c) Savings and bank accounts and amounts.
   d) Personal property and household furnishings and their value, including automobiles, boats, etc.
   e) Objects of art, stamp, coin, gun, or other collections and their value.

f) Pension or profit-sharing plans to which the testator may have rights.
g) Life insurance (policy numbers, amounts, and company names) payable upon the testator's death, and all annuities (monthly payment plans).
h) A listing of all the testator's business interests if any, value, etc., including copyrights or patents.

The lawyer should have a list of major debts or obligations of the testator; that is, mortgage obligations, long-term debt, automobile payments, homeowners insurance premiums, etc. Depending somewhat on the nature or extent of the testator's estate, holdings, or interests, the lawyer may need or wish to know the names and addresses of the testator's accountant, bank officer, stock broker, insurance broker, or others who can provide information if needed.

What Your Will Should Include

Partly by your writing down specific details or bequests you wish to include in your will, and partly by your discussions with your attorney, your attorney will secure the information he needs to draw the will.

If your estate is not complicated or you have no special bequests, it could be as simple as a will left by Calvin Coolidge, which simply said, "I leave everything to my wife," and named her as executor. However, most wills need to be more extensive and should provide for all foreseeable contingencies. Here are details you should consider:

Real Estate:
Real property may be left outright to a specific beneficiary or it may be placed in trust to provide either income or a place of residence for the family or other beneficiaries. If the property is to be sold, the proceeds can become part of the general

estate or left to specific beneficiaries. If he wishes, the testator can grant a *life-estate* to a beneficiary; that is, a right for the beneficiary to live in the property or use it for life. Upon the death of the beneficiary, ownership would shift to someone else as directed by the will. Often, disposition of property is left to the discretion of the executor.

Cash Bequests:

Cash bequests in the will may or may not create problems. If the will directs that certain specific dollar amounts be made to certain beneficiaries or charitable groups, the executor may have to sell property or other items to obtain the needed cash. If the estate turns out to be less than the testator anticipated, the cash bequests may reduce the remainder of the estate to a lesser amount than the testator had wanted or intended for certain other beneficiaries who were not left specific bequests. If such a potential exists, a better method would be for the testator to leave a certain percentage of the estate to specified beneficiaries or groups.

Personal Property:

If all personal belongings are left to one person such as the spouse, the will should so state and the items will pass to that person and usually there are no special problems. However, if the testator wishes an automobile, a stamp collection, a set of golf clubs, etc. to go to a particular person, the will must set forth the specific bequest. The will should clearly set forth the testator's desires to avoid family dissension.

The Estate Remainder:

After all specific bequests have been distributed or provided for, the balance left is called the estate remainder or residual. In his will the testator should state exactly how this remainder is to be disposed. He may leave it entirely to his (or her) spouse with no further restrictions or stipulations. However, he may wish to set up a trust fund with the income to go to his wife's (and/or children's) support and for her health and wellbeing. The trustee may also be authorized to use money from the principal if needed. If the estate is to be divided between two or more persons, the will should state exactly the portions each is to receive; that is, $1/2$ to A, $1/4$ to B, $1/4$ to C, etc.

Guardian For Minor Children:

If assets are to be left to minor children, the best method is for the testator to name a guardian in his will. In the absence of such a provision, the court will name a guardian to protect the children and their property. A spouse, of course, may be named as the guardian of the children's property or often a bank or trust company is so named. The guardian is empowered to use the property for the children's support, health, wellbeing, and education. Usually the property is to be turned over to a child when he or she reaches age 21 or other stipulated age.

The Executor

The executor, or executrix, is the person named in the will to administer the estate. He or she is the person who assembles all the decedent's (the person who died) assets, pays all debts, temporarily manages and invests the property, pays out all taxes, files necessary tax or legal forms, and then, when all of these matters are completed, distributes the remaining estate to the beneficiaries. The executor could be a spouse, a relative, or close friend. However, unless the estate is relatively small and uncomplicated it is often best to use the trust office of a bank or an experienced estate lawyer. If the decedent died without a will, the probate court will appoint an administrator.

Executors or administrators are known as fiduciaries. Fiduararies must take great care in dealing with the decedent's property. They must take greater care than they do with their own property. Fiduciaries usually are paid a commission established by statute but this fee can be waived. The more complicated an estate, the more important it is to have an executor who is experienced in estate matters. Your lawyer may be a good choice if you have complete trust in him. If the executor is not a lawyer (or a bank trust department), the executor should work closely with the family lawyer to make certain all legal matters are properly handled.

Changing Your Will

Before you die, you may revoke or change your will freely at anytime. The easiest and most common way to revoke a will is simply to execute a new one that expressly revokes any previous ones. A will may also be cancelled just by tearing it up and throwing it away.

A will may also be changed by amendment. This amendment is called a *codicil*. A codicil is for the purpose of changing a particular portion of the will and must be executed with the same formality as the original will. Generally, it is better and just about as easy to type a whole new will which readily can be done in the lawyer's office on word processors.

If You Die Without a Will

If a person dies with no will or has left an invalid will, he is said to have died *intestate*. In such a case, the probate court will appoint an administrator who is subject to strict legal rules and fiduciary conduct of a highly conservative nature.

Established by the state, there is a priority of inheritance within the family where there is no will. This priority is called "intestate succession." All states provide for division of the property among spouses and children. Although there is some variation, the spouse usually receives one-third to one-half and the children receive the remainder. Should there be no surviving spouse, the children receive it all. In some states if there are no children, the spouse receives it all. However, in most states, the estate is divided between the spouse and the decedent's surviving parents. If there is neither a surviving spouse or children, the parents receive it all, and if no surviving parents, brothers and sisters or their issue receive all. If there are no known relatives who qualify, the estate may go to the state in which the decedent lived.

Property Rights of The Spouse

Every state has laws which protect the rights of a surviving spouse in the property of a deceased spouse. There are a wide variety of state laws, but basically the laws fall into four categories.

1) All states have "exempt properties" such as household effects and small sums of money. The spouse has a priority to these items and the right to their use.

2) Some states have special rights relating to real estate. These rights are called *dower rights* for women and *curtesy rights* for men. In states where they apply, these rights mean that the spouse has a one-third ownership right or share in real property. Both dower and curtesy apply in some states and in some states only dower rights. Check with your lawyer or state to determine what applies in your state.

3) Most states provide that a spouse may take a "statutory share" of the estate instead of what was provided in the will. The amount that may be taken is usually about the same as that which would have been allowed if the person died with no will. Usually, this share is one-third of the total estate, or it may be the right to the income from a

trust of one-third of the assets plus a certain amount of cash.

4) A few states have *community property* laws, also called *marital property* laws. Under these laws each spouse owns one-half of all property they have acquired while married, except for inheritances or gifts. When a spouse dies, the surviving spouse already owns one-half of their marital property. In his will, the decedent may also further provide for the survivor by leaving him or her all or part of his own separate property.

Laws pertaining to inheritance rights are varied and complicated. The law of the state in which you live governs. Consult with your lawyer to avoid misunderstandings and legal difficulties.

Probate

Probate is the legal procedure which approves the distribution of the property of a person's estate. It is simply the process of proving the validity of a person's will. When validity has been proven, the will becomes a matter of public record. If there is no will, the estate will be distributed according to the laws of the state.

Probate procedure is generally routine. It is accomplished simply by the filing of affidavits signed by the witnesses stating that the will was signed by the decedent knowingly, voluntarily, and apparently in sound mind. If there is a challenge to the will, the probate judge must determine the legality of the challenge and what procedures are to be followed.

As mentioned earlier, if there is no will, the probate judge will appoint an administrator who performs the same function as an executor. If an executor was named in the will, he must be approved by the court as being eligible under the laws of the state. If he is approved, the court issues a document which states that the person named is authorized to administer the estate. The probate court administers an oath to the executor (administrator), who must swear to perform his duties faithfully.

Note: Depending on the complexity of the estate, the executor's duties can be detailed and complex. The executor, if not a lawyer or experienced in estate handling, must work closely with a lawyer and familiarize himself with his responsibilities and legal obligations.

Chapter 9
CONSUMER PROTECTION*

Both Congress and state legislatures have passed laws to protect the consumer. The protection provided is based on the theory that the consumer cannot easily protect himself from many illegal or unfair practices. If a person does not know or have any way of telling that a scheme or a statement is deceptive, he can do little to avoid the results.

However, you can do much to learn to recognize deceptive schemes and practices and thereby to avoid them. In addition, if you have a knowledge or understanding of consumer protective law, you will know when you can take legal action and when you should file a complaint with a state or federal agency.

Some of the principal areas where protective laws have been passed concern the following:

1) Deceptive advertising

2) Deceptive sales methods

3) Improper Collection Methods

Deceptive Advertising

The test of whether or not advertising is deceptive is whether the buyer was misled regardless of the intent or lack of intent on the part of the seller. In the past, only if the buyer committed an intentional fraudulent act did the consumer have a remedy. But today, the seller must be able to show that his advertising was reasonable, true, and fair.

Various governmental agencies have the responsibility of policing or regulating advertising practices. The Federal Trade Commission polices retail advertising to determine whether the advertising is true or correct and whether or not the consumer might be misled. The Public Health Smoking Act makes

---

* See Canadian Law, page 102.

the Surgeon General's office responsible for seeing that proper warning notices appear on each cigarette package and in print advertising. Cigarette advertising has been banned on radio and television. Other agencies have other responsibilities.

Advertisers are required to maintain records or have proof of any statements or claims they make about their product — its quality, its contents, its safety, or other factors. As a consumer, pay attention to the advertising you see or hear. Analyze what is being stated. If you feel claims or statements are deceiving, you have a right to complain. In some cases, if you have relied on the claims, expressed or implied, and you are injured, you may have a right to file for a remedy under tort law against the advertiser.

Bait and Switch:

The bait and switch tactic is not so common as it was formerly, but it still occurs. Most state laws and FTC regulations prohibit such tactics.

In one version of this scheme, the advertiser offers an item at a very low price. In other words, he "baits" the customer. Then, when the customer comes to the store, a salesman attempts to "switch" the customer to some other, usually higher priced, item or article. Often he disparges the sale item, so the buyer is discouraged from buying it. This practice has often been used by non-reputable stores or dealers to sell television sets, appliances, pianos, etc. The low-cost item is disparged or "talked down" in favor of the higher-priced item. In the case of automobiles, the seller may say or claim the automobile has already been sold.

It should be noted, however, it is perfectly legal to try to "trade-up" a customer. It is a legitimate trade-up if the advertiser has a sufficient number of the advertised items in stock and will sell them willingly. The salesman may attempt to sell the advantages of a higher-priced item, but he does not disparge the advertised item. In such a case, the trading-up tactic is legitimate. Sometimes there is a fine line between "bait-and-switch" and "trade-up."

Another version of this same tactic is to advertise a "special price" usually on a well-known, regular item. But the store does not have sufficient stock to meet the demand. The store knows the buyer will often take something else and probably buy other items as well. Although outlawed, the practice continues. Reputable stores, if they run out of stock, will usually give "rain checks," so that the buyer can later secure the item at the special price; or they state in their advertising "while supply lasts."

Some states prohibit "fire sales," "water damage sales," "going out of business sales," unless these events have occurred or are taking place. The laws of many states or other jurisdictions require a special license to conduct such sales to assure the customer they are legitimate.

Deceptive Packaging or Labeling

The Fair Products Labeling Act requires that products bear a label that identifies the product, the name and address of the manufacturer, the packer or distributor, the net quantity of the total contents, and the net quantity of one serving if the number of servings is stated on the label. Depending on the product, other disclosures may be required.

The federal Food and Drug Administration regulates the labeling and packaging of food, drugs, and cosmetics. Unwarranted claims for a product's use cannot be made. In addition, warnings as to a product's use or frequency of use must be clearly stated.

For clothing and other items, countries of origin or manufacture must be given. Flammable fabrics cannot be used for certain products. Cleaning instructions should be given if the garment requires certain care. Deceptive terms such as giant size, jumbo size, family size are forbidden in some cases by

state and federal laws where such terms create the impression
that more is contained in the package than is really the case.

Product Approvals:

The labels or tags on many products indicate they have been
tested or approved by some organization or agency. This test-
ing or approval indicates that the product has been manufactured according to certain safety or quality standards and that
the consumer can be assured that the product is safe or of good
quality.

Such an approval normally carries only the liability to refund
the price or to replace a defective article. However, if the
buyer is injured in any way by the article or its use, the approval
agency, the manufacturer, and the seller may all be held liable
under an implied or express warranty or other provisions of
tort law. In case of injury, it is usually best to consult an
attorney.

Deceptive Selling Methods

The law seeks to protect the consumer and to punish those
who conduct fraudulent or unlawful selling practices. Earlier,
under *Deceptive Advertising*, the "Bait and Switch" method
was discussed. Other provisions concerning selling methods
are presented here.

Deceptive Pricing:

Guidelines established by the Federal Trade Commission
prohibit advertising or sales methods that cause the customer
to believe that he is buying an item for substantially less than
the customary price. For example, a store places an item that
cost the store $10 on its shelf for a short time at a price of
$50. It does not really expect to sell many, if any, at that
price. A week or two later, they run an ad saying, "Price
slashed 50%. Was $50, now only $25." Unless the store has

actually sold a reasonable quantity at the $50 price, they have made a false claim and would be in violation of the guidelines.

The use of the term "wholesale" is also a deceptive practice and may be used only by bona fide wholesalers selling to bona fide retailers. If the prices quoted by a so called wholesaler are not really wholesale, he may be subject to legal proceedings by the FTC. If you see an ad that says, "At or below wholesale," investigate carefully. There are times when the quoted price may be even higher than normal retail.

Sometimes an ad or a tag quotes a suggested manufacturer's price and then gives a lower price. This practice is deceptive if the seller claims his price is substantially less than *normal retail* when in fact it is not. If the price is usually and normally the retail price stated, his reduced price claim is legitimate. However, if the item bears a suggested retail price but normally, in the subject store and other stores the item sells for less, the pricing claim is deceptive.

Shop around and compare prices and claims for any price reductions. If you find or feel the pricing of an item is deceptive, file a complaint with some authority. This authority could be a local or state agency, the Federal Trade Commission, or the Better Business Bureau.

Door-to-door Sales:

Because of unfair, deceptive, or high-pressure door-to-door sales practices, the Federal Trade Commission has issued regulations prohibiting many practices and providing customers with a decision period. During the period provided, the individual can determine whether or not he really wishes to buy the merchandise or subscribe to the service. Under FTC orders, specified companies must:

1) Inform the purchaser that he has three days in which to cancel the order;

2) Provide cancellation forms which the buyer can complete and return;

3) Cannot assign the instrument of debt to a bank or other institution until five days after the date of sale.

Mail-order Sales:

If the mails are used to defraud, federal laws protect the customer. State statutes also forbid deceptive practices. As is true for door-to-door sales, the consumer has certain rights:

1) To know when he can expect to receive the merchandise;

2) To have the merchandise shipped within 30 days;

3) To be notified and to be provided with a free means of reply if there is to be a delay;

4) To agree to a new shipping date;

5) To have all payments returned if 30 days elapse and the merchandise has not been shipped.

Unsolicited Merchandise:

Federal law prohibits the shipment of unsolicited merchandise to a person's home. If such goods are received, the recipient may keep the unordered goods and use them or dispose of them in any way he wishes. In addition, the seller is prohibited from mailing an invoice for the merchandise.

There are two exceptions to this rule: 1) free samples clearly marked as such, and 2) items (such as Christmas cards, pens, labels) mailed by charitable organizations asking for a contribution. The individual is not obligated to send a contribution nor to return the items.

Improper Collection Methods

To force slow-paying customers to pay their debts, some

companies have used false representations or abusive tactics. Some have sent documents that appear to be legal forms or court summons that make it appear as if a law suit had been filed.

Many such practices have been prohibited by the Fair Debt Collection Practices Act of 1977. Enforced by the FTC, the act's purpose is to ensure that people are treated fairly by debt collectors.

Under the Act, any deceptive method of debt collection is illegal. If the methods used are unreasonable, the methods may involve the invasion of the individuals *right of privacy* and may be justification for the debtor to bring legal action. Among the specific practices prohibited by the Act are:

1) Notifying a debtor's employer of a debt;

2) Using the telephone to harass the debtor and his family;

3) Hiring private investigators or others to follow, embarrass, or intimidate the debtor.

If you are subject to abusive collection or billing tactics, you should notify the FTC or consult with your attorney. If the deceptive practices are being engaged in by a financial institution licensed by the state, the licensing state agency should be notified.

Legal Remedies Against Deception

The legal remedies available to the consumer who has been duped by deceptive advertising or selling methods are not always practical or too effective. In case of actual injury, the main course against a company or business is to sue for fraud. However, there are two difficulties in this approach: 1) the cost of the litigation, and 2) the difficulty of proving the fraud.

Usually, the total amount involved does not exceed $500,

and the cost of the litigation could easily exceed this amount. If negotiation with the merchant (or pressure brought by an outside agency) does not succeed, the individual may well have to "chalk it up to experience." In order to win a court case, the plaintiff must prove that the seller *made* a false representation, that the seller *knew* the representation was false, and that he, the buyer, *relied* on the false statement in making his purchase. Proving these facts is often exceedingly difficult.

The Federal Trade Commission was established to limit unfair methods of competition. However, they can only investigate practices which are "in the public interest." The FTC cannot and will not intervene in a purely private controversy. They will not intervene unless the practice seems to be a part of a company's general practice or conduct of business, and it is, therefore, in the public interest to stop the practice.

How You Can Protect Yourself

As can be seen, there is sometimes little you can do about small individual losses, but to protect yourself be fully informed about the practices discussed in this section so that you recognize their use. To combat the deceptive practices here are five rules:

1) Shop intelligently.
Here is where your knowledge of deceptive practices will come into play. With this knowledge you can recognize deceptive practices, avoid their use or effectiveness on you, and find legitimate good buys with reputable firms.

2) Report complaints to consumer protection agencies.
At times you may have to chalk a transaction "up to experience." But don't take things sitting down. Discuss the problem with the merchant. If you get no satisfaction complain to the Better Business Bureau, to the state consumer affairs department, etc.

3) *Complain to the news media.*

If you complain to the news media (radio, television, magazines, or newspapers) where the merchant advertises, the media may investigate. If enough people complain, they may refuse to accept additional advertising from the advertiser. Writing to "Action Lines" in newspapers often does bring action.

4) *Complain to local or state enforcement agencies.*

Most states have deceptive advertising laws and many enforce them vigorously. If you have a complaint, consult with local enforcement agencies such as the county attorney or state attorney general.

5) *Write to the Federal Trade Commission.*

Use discretion in writing to the FTC. As mentioned they cannot intervene in private controversies particularly of an isolated or local issue. However, they have broad responsibility to halt unfair methods of competition or deceptive practices in commerce if the situation has "sufficient public interest." If you feel the advertising of a company is deceptive, if door-to-door sales people are violating the rules that you know are in force, if a mail order company fails to make a legitimate refund after several requests, file a complaint with the FTC. They will determine if it is the public interest to investigate further.

By recognizing deceptive practices, you can detect, avoid, and help curtail or prevent deceptive advertising and selling methods. If you have been injured or have a complaint that involves a substantial amount of money, you should consult your lawyer. In other cases, complaint to a city, state, or federal agency may bring action.

Chapter 10
WHEN YOU NEED A LAWYER

Law is complex. Most of the time you can conduct your personal affairs without a lawyer. But it is important to know when you need a lawyer and when you do not. Unfortunately, many of us delay in consulting a lawyer until we are in serious trouble and need one in a hurry.

In the preceding sections, information has been presented that should enable you to recognize many legal difficulties that may arise. Being aware that there may be a legal problem enables you to know the consequences of signing a contract or of being negligent or careless. However, there are situations when you will need legal advice to fully understand a personal or business situation. A good lawyer can help you avoid legal pitfalls and prevent you from taking a legally unwise action.

Hiring a Lawyer

If you are accused of a crime you clearly need a lawyer. You need one if you are purchasing a home or other property, engaged in a marital dispute, sued for a personal injury, entering into a major business arrangement or construction project, arrested for drunken driving, and many, many other situations.

But often, you don't just need any lawyer. You need a lawyer who has a good knowledge of and specializes in the field of your particular legal problem. For example, if you are being sued for personal injury you don't need or want an attorney that specializes in copyright law.

Here is a general breakdown of some of the different areas or types of law in which lawyers tend to specialize. Large legal firms will usually have individual lawyers who are specialists in many of these areas. However, if you engage a small firm or single lawyer, be sure they or he is experienced in your particular problem.

Areas of Specialization

Civil Trial Law

If you are suing or being sued for breach of contract, involved in a property dispute, involved in a will contest, etc., you need a civil trial lawyer.

Business or Corporate Law

Lawyers or firms who specialize in business law may (or may not) be the same as those engaged in civil trial law. If you need a major business contract prepared, particularly if substantial sums of money are involved, if you plan to buy or sell a business, enter into a joint venture or partnership, you need an experienced business law attorney.

Civil Law

Again, a civil lawyer may or may not be a civil trial lawyer or a business lawyer. In general, a civil lawyer handles real estate purchase and sales agreements, drafts contracts of various types, interprets contracts and other documents such as insurance policies, government agency regulations, etc.

Personal Injury Law

Personal injury or accident lawyers are civil trial lawyers but specialize in injury cases including malpractice suits.

Marital Relations Law

Again, marital relations lawyers are civil trial lawyers, but they specialize in handling divorces, separation agreements, child custody, adoptions, etc.

Will Preparation, Estate Planning, and Probate Law

There are civil law lawyers who specialize in drafting wills, preparing trusts, acting as executors, trustees, or guardians, etc. Some bank trust departments also perform these functions.

Criminal Law

If you are ever accused or arrested for a crime, including drunk driving, immediately hire an experienced criminal lawyer. A good divorce lawyer will not do.

As indicated by the preceding, there are definite legal specialties, although some lawyers are competent and experienced in more than one of the areas given. The important thing is that you get a firm or lawyer highly knowledgeable in your particular legal problem. Other areas of specialization include the following:

1) Tax law

2) Immigration law

3) Patent, copyright, and trademark law

When Do You Need a Lawyer?

There are many legal problems that are so minor that employing a lawyer would not be warranted; for example, a dispute over a $50 repair bill. Often a complaint or a problem should be presented to a governmental agency, consumer protection agency, or law enforcement agency. However, there are times when it is essential that you should consult and engage a lawyer. These include:

1) Buying, selling, or building a house or building

2) Making or terminating a lease other than for routine apartment rental

3) Securing an opinion on a real estate title

4) Accidents where you have been injured or may be liable for injury to others or where claims have been filed

5) Property damage problems

6) Marital disputes which may result in divorce, separation, child custody, etc.

7) Adoptions

8) When arrested or accused of a crime

9) Planning an estate; will preparation

10) Deaths; estate administration

11) Major landlord difficulties

12) Tax disputes or problems

13) Preparation or examination of contracts involving reasonable amounts of money or involving other legal problems

14) Organizing, buying, selling or dissolving a business, partnership, or joint venture

15) Contract disputes; fraud; deceit; defamation

16) Employee-employer problems

17) Debt collection or other business problems

18) Dealing with governmental agencies on serious or complicated matters

19) Major consumer problems

20) Taking out copyrights, patents, or trademarks

21) Violation of one's personal rights, sexual harassment, etc.

22) Serious money problems

How To Find A Good Lawyer

Often, the best way to locate a lawyer is through the recommendation of your employer, a business associate, a good friend or anyone else you respect or trust. A doctor, minister, or accountant also may be able to help you.

Going to a large well-known legal firm may be good, but such a firm may be more costly than a smaller firm or individual attorney. Legal directories are a good source and are available in law libraries or in many public or university libraries. For example, the *Martindale-Hubbell Law Directory* is arranged geographically, gives information on lawyers in every sizable community in the country, and for some lawyers gives a listing of specialties.

If you call your local bar association and tell them your legal problem, they can recommend two to five lawyers who specialize in or are competent to handle your problem. But however you secure the name of a lawyer, you must then interview him or her and decide if he or she is right for you.

If you cannot afford to hire a lawyer, go to the Legal Aid Society or the local bar association. They can provide you with information on free or low cost legal sources. Unions, the American Civil Liberties Union, or organizations such as the NAACP or senior citizen groups may also be of help. The Women's Legal Defense Fund provides services for women with problems in domestic relations or sex discrimination.

Your First Meeting

On your first meeting with a lawyer, you must decide on whether or not you wish to hire him or her. For a lawyer to be good for you, you must have confidence in him and feel comfortable in dealing and talking with him. Here are some points to consider in establishing your relationship and making your decision.

1) Before going to the meeting, make notes of all the important aspects of the problem so that you can remember

to discuss them with the lawyer, or even to give him a copy of your notes.

2) Assemble and bring with you all written papers or documents that pertain to the case. Have the names, addresses and telephone numbers of anyone connected with the case.

3) Ask the lawyer what experience he has in dealing with cases exactly like or very similar to yours. If dealing with a law firm, will the person you are talking to be handling your case or will someone else? If someone else, you should meet and talk to the other lawyer as well.

4) If the lawyer says something that is not clear to you, ask for a further explanation. Don't hesitate to ask questions.

Your hiring decision should be based on whether or not you feel comfortable with the lawyer; does he seem to have the particular skill or experience that you need for your type of case, and is the fee reasonable or acceptable to you? If you say "no" to any of these factors, you may not wish to hire him.

Keep in mind, the lawyer may or may not particularly want you as a client. Have you been completely open and honest with him or are you holdng back some facts? Are you willing to largely depend on his advice as to the conduct of the case?

The majority of cases do not end up in court. Exceptions are when you are being sued or being arrested for a crime. In many civil cases, the lawyer may feel that a court suit would be futile, and he may recommend further negotiation or some compromise. To a large degree, if you hire him you must follow or should follow his counsel and advice.

Prior Fee Understanding

Talk openly and frankly with your prospective lawyer about

the fees he may charge or the expenses you may face. Fees vary greatly depending on the time and the services the lawyer may have to provide. Fees also vary from one area to another and from one lawyer to another. Do not be hesitant to ask about fees. Rules of the American Bar Association specifically urge attorneys to have a prior or written fee understanding with their clients. Here are some of the factors that may determine the fee in a particular case:

1) The fee normally charged in that particular community for that particular type of case.

2) The amount of time the lawyer may have to spend. (The fee may be based on an hourly rate and therefore dependant on the number of hours spent.)

3) The reputation, the experience, the skills of the lawyer employed. (The greater his reputation or skills, the greater his fee.)

4) Whether the fee is a fixed amount or a contingent fee. (If the fee is contingent, the lawyer receives nothing unless he wins the case.)

5) The nature of a relationship with a client. (A client coming in for a first-time and possibly a one-time case, normally would be charged a higher rate compared to a client who has regularly used the lawyer's services.)

Getting What You Pay For

There are legal firms with many lawyers and large support staffs that tend to service wealthy individuals or corporations and charge high fees. However, there are diligent capable lawyers who can assist you and serve you no matter what your economic means.

Your particular case may not warrant the expense of hiring

the most expensive legal firm or lawyer. If you are engaging a lawyer for a routine drafting of a contract, a debt collection, a dispute with your landlord, there are many small firms or individual lawyers that can do an excellent, low-cost representation for you.

Specialized lawyers are needed and best for criminal cases, civil trial cases, divorce cases, tax cases, and for immigration, copyright, patent, bankruptcy, or other similar legal situations. General legal firms with small legal staffs and practices can often do an excellent job for you.

Chapter 11
CANADIAN LAW

Types of Law

In Canada, by virtue of the Constitution Act of 1867, the legislatures of the various provinces have vested in them sole jurisdiction over certain matters, such as property law. Jurisdiction over remaining matters, such as criminal law, is vested in the federal Parliament. The provincial legislatures in turn have delegated certain legislative powers to municipalities for the purposes of self-government.

There are two sources of law in Canada: common law and statute law.

The bulk of Canadian law is common law, so named because it is derived from the Common Law of the Realm in England, a collection of the laws of the various counties which were common to all. Because it is founded on the decisions of judges, it is also referred to at times as case law. The primary characteristic of common law is that it is based on precedent in that the decision of a court is binding on all inferior courts until it is reversed or distinguished by a court of a higher jurisdiction. It should be noted that the laws of Quebec, because of its French heritage, instead of being based on the Common Law of the Realm, is based on the old French law and the Napoleonic Code.

Statute law is comprised of all Acts of any legislature. Because common law is based on precedent, changes or additions to common law are generally accomplished through statute law.

No-fault Liability

Chapter 2 presented information on intentional or negligent conduct which causes harm. In some areas of law, as in laws concerning motor vehicle accidents, Canadian law is moving towards no-fault liability; that is, that there is legal liability without fault. In other words, legal liability will attach to a party without the necessity of showing that the party has intentionally interfered with another person or his property or of showing that the person has not followed reasonable standards of care.

Contracts That Must Be in Writing

The Canadian Statute of Frauds, which is in force in forms in all common law provinces, except Manitoba, provides that certain types of contracts are unenforceable by action in a court of law, unless they are evidenced by some memorandum or note in writing signed by the person to be charged. Although the legislation differs from province to province, those types of contracts commonly required to be in writing are as follows:
1) A contract by the executor or administrator of an estate to discharge personally the debt or obligation of the estate;
2) A contract of guarantee;
3) An agreement made in consideration of marriage;
4) A contract for the sale or other disposition of land or interest in land, including long term leases;
5) An agreement which is not to be performed within one year from the time of the agreement.

Unenforceable Contracts
In Canada, Indians on reservations are protected from certain types of liability.

Specific Performance
A contract for personal services is not specifically enforceable.

Property Title

Title to property is conveyed under a Deed or Transfer from the Seller to the Buyer. The contract for sale will usually provide that the Seller is to convey fee simple title. This is the highest form of title.

When the Buyer is more than one person, title can be taken as joint tenants or as tenants in common. If it is desired that title be taken as joint tenants, this must be specifically mentioned in the Deed or Transfer as otherwise the law presumes that title is taken as tenants in common. Joint tenancy is marked by the characteristic of survivorship, that is, upon the death of one joint tenant, the entire tenancy goes to the survivors, and so on until the last survivor.

Final Closing—Property

In Canada, the closing or completion of the transaction will take place on the date specified in the contract. Usually the closing will take place at the Registry Office for the municipality where the property is situated. The Deed or Transfer and keys are delivered to the solicitor for the Buyer and the balance of the purchase price is delivered to the solicitor for the Seller. The solicitor for the Buyer also registers the Deed or Transfer in the records of ownership at the Registry Office.

Residential Tenancy Legislation

All provinces in Canada have some type of residential tenancy legislation designed to protect the rights of tenants and to provide tenants with some sort of protection against the advantage which landlords may have by virtue of the landlord-tenant relationship.

A landlord may not obtain a security deposit against performance of an obligation by the tenant other than the obligation to pay rent. Therefore it is not permitted to take security deposits, key deposits, commissions or any extra sums except for the payment in advance of the last month's rent. Generally, a landlord cannot insist on the delivery of postdated cheques by a tenant for rental payments. Generally there are limits to the increases which may be charged to a tenant by a landlord. The maximum increase differs from province to province but fluctuates between 4 and 10 percent.

Termination of Tenancies

A tenant is entitled to terminate his tenancy at the end of his term so long as he gives the notice required by the applicable legislation. A tenancy renews itself automatically if no notice is provided.

A landlord tends to have fewer opportunities to terminate a tenant's term of tenancy and must usually give more notice, except in the case of nonpayment of rent, usually two or three months. Causes, other than nonpayment of rent, which may give rise to a right to terminate the tenancy include illegal activity on the premises, failing to repair damage caused by the tenant or his guests, and overcrowding.

Generally the applicable legislation requires that a landlord may not regain possession of leased premises against the will of a tenant unless under a writ of possession authorized by a court of competent jurisdiction.

Employment Provisions

Each Canadian province has laws that establish certain minimum standards of employment. These standards generally include the following:

1) Maximum number of hours an employee can work in a week.

2) Number of hours after which employee must be paid overtime.

3) Minimum wages.

4) Employers must give employees certain days, including Christmas Day, Good Friday, Labour Day and New Year's Day, as a holiday with pay.

5) An employee must be given at least two weeks' vacation with pay.

6) Employers are required to give employees one day off per week.

7) A forum for an employee to file a grievance against an employer for non-compliance with legal requirements.

8) An employee must be given notice of termination or pay in lieu thereof unless there is cause for termination.

Human Rights Legislation

All Canadian jurisdictions have enacted human rights legislation designed to ensure that certain values considered fundamental are maintained at all times. This legislation contains the following material aspects:

1) Prohibition of discrimination on the basis of race, creed, colour, age, sex, marital status, citizenship, ancestry, place of origin, ethnic origin, family status or handicap in employment practices such as hiring, firing, training, promoting and conditions of employment.

2) Equal pay for women and men for equal work.

3) A forum for handling of complaints based on non-compliance.

Social Security

The federal government offers two types of retirement benefits: the Canada Pension Plan and the Old Age Security Pension.

The Canada (and accompanying Quebec) Pension Plan require mandatory contributions from employers and employees, including self-employed individuals. Contributions are related to earnings. Benefits are also related to earnings and are indexed to offset inflation.

Benefits include a retirement pension beginning at any time between ages sixty and seventy, a disability pension provided the disability is total, and survivor benefits for spouses and orphans.

Old Age Security is a universal pension payable from age sixty-five subject to residency requirements.

Family Property and Married Persons' Property Rights

The common law deemed the husband and wife to be one person and the person represented that person. Statute law has now made husbands and wives separate individuals at law.

The basic concept in the common law provinces is that of separate property. A woman has the capacity to own property separately from her husband. Property brought into the marriage by one spouse remains the property of that spouse. Property acquired during the marriage belongs to the person who paid for it.

However the concept of separate property gives rise to problems because the concept does not take into account the notion of marriage as a partnership with the husband providing the income and the wife acting as a homemaker. Even if both spouses work, the reality is that the family is one economic unit. Therefore legislation has been introduced which basically provides that property which is acquired by one spouse is still controlled by that spouse and may be sold or otherwise dealt with during the continuance of the marriage. Upon separation, either spouse may apply to a court for a sharing of certain assets, called family or matrimonial assets.

An application may be made for the division of these assets when there is divorce or where the parties are separated and there is no reasonable prospect of resumption of cohabitation.

The assets which are to be shared differ according to the applicable legislation but generally include all property acquired during cohabitation together with the matrimonial home. Generally, the court will award each spouse an equal share in the family or matrimonial assets unless it is of the opinion that the division along these lines would be unfair.

The scheme of sharing upon marital breakdown can be altered by contract between the spouses. The scheme for division of assets upon breakdown of a relationshp does not apply to parties who are living together but are not married to each other.

The matrimonial home is the property occupied by a married person and his or her spouse as their family residence.

Generally, the applicable legislation provides that each spouse has a right to possession of the matrimonial home and that neither spouse can dispose of or give a mortgage on the matrimonial home, even if that spouse is the sole owner, without the consent of the other spouse.

In all common law provinces, either spouse may apply for exclusive possession of the matrimonial home. Generally, such an order is granted by a court if it is considered to be in the best interest of a child to the marriage. For instance, such an order may be made if other provision for shelter is considered not to be adequate in the opinion of the court.

CANADIAN LAW

Types of Wills

The following are the types of wills that can be valid under Canadian law:

1) The English form of will must be in writing and signed at the end by the testator. The signature must be made or acknowledged by the testator in the presence of two or more witnesses present at the same time.

2) A notarial will is valid only if it is made in Quebec. It must be made before two notaries or before one notary and two witnesses.

3) A holograph will is valid under the law of every Canadian jurisdiction but British Columbia, Prince Edward Island, and Nova Scotia. This is a will written by the testator in his or her own handwriting. No witnesses are required. The entire will must be in the testator's own handwriting.

4) Under the Convention Providing a Uniform Law on the Form of an International Will, there is set out the formal requirements for a valid international will and an authorized person attaches a certificate establishing that the legal requirements of the Convention have been complied with. This type of will is legal in Alberta, Manitoba, Newfoundland, and Ontario.

Consumer Protection

Legislation has been passed in recent years dealing with several areas of concern in the area of consumer protection. This legislation includes the following:

1) Misleading and inaccurate representations made by sellers to consumers.

2) Safety of consumer products.

3) Deceptive sale methods.

Each of the provincial legislatures has enacted two types of consumer protection legislation. First there is legislation aimed at regulating the techniques used to sell goods and services to consumers. Secondly, there is legislation aimed at redressing unfairness in individual consumer transactions.

Some points raised in such legislation are the following:

1) Where a contract has been signed with an itinerant seller, such a contract may be voided within two days of being signed provided that all goods received under the contract are returned promptly.

2) A buyer to whom credit is extended must be supplied with a written statement showing the cost of borrowing.

3) A consumer who receives unsolicited goods need not pay for them. Such goods include an unsolicited credit card.

4) An agreement to purchase goods may be cancelled if such agreement is a result of false, misleading or deceptive representations or as a result of unconscionable consumer representations.

5) Individuals engaged in certain categories of businesses, such as mortgage brokers or real estate agents, must be licensed.

Types of consumer legislation not previously mentioned are:

1) Consumer packaging and labelling legislation;

2) Food and drug legislation;

3) National trade mark and labelling legislation;

4) Textile labelling legislation;

5) Hazardous product legislation;

6) Motor vehicle safety legislation.

NOTES

NOTES

NOTES

NOTES

NOTES

NOTES

NOTES

NOTES

NOTES

NOTES